GrossyPelosi is famously the hostess with the mostest—now it's your turn to invite everyone in.

Dan Pelosi believes every day can be a celebration—and wherever there's a celebration, there's a menu waiting to be planned. In his second cookbook, the *New York Times* bestselling author dishes out more than 100 of his larger-than-life recipes, organized into sixteen distinct dinner parties designed to take the guesswork out of what to serve when and what goes with what. Some celebrations are familiar, like *Giving Thanks* (but—surprise!—we're having roast chicken), and others prove any time calls for entertaining: *Breakfast for Dinner* makes your pajamas party-worthy with **RAISIN WALNUT BAKED FRENCH TOAST** (which you can assemble ahead of time). The menus and recipes will carry you through every season of life, and of the year, too: When the sun comes out, lay out by the pool with **BEANY BIKINI DIP** or cool off with no-cook-tomato-sauce **SUNSHINE PASTA**. After the showers bring forth flowers, carve out a night for **LAMB CHOPS WITH TANGY APRICOT SAUCE**, one of Bimpy's forever favorites. Bet you never thought of **PUMPKIN CIDER BRAISED PORK SHOULDER** as a way to get your seasonal spice fix! And, of course, you'll know when it's time to preheat your oven to replicate Dan's iconic *Holiday Cookie Party*.

Whether you follow a menu as is or mix and match recipes, Dan helps you find the joy in every part of hosting, from setting the guest list to politely letting your company know when it's time to go home, sharing his favorite family tidbits along the way (including his dad's guide for Italian American slang—capisce?). For seasoned hosts and first-timers alike, this book is your manual. Save the date, dress up the table, and choose your outfit . . . now *LET'S PARTY!*

Let's Party

LET'S PARTY

Recipes and
Menus for
Celebrating
Every Day

UNION
SQUARE
& CO.

NEW YORK

DAN PELOSI

PHOTOGRAPHS BY JOHNNY MILLER

UNION
SQUARE
& CO.

NEW YORK

●●●

Text © 2025 Dan Pelosi
Photographs © 2025 Johnny Miller

ISBN 978-1-4549-5678-5
ISBN 978-1-4549-5679-2 (e-book)

Union Square & Co. books may be purchased in bulk for business, educational, or promotional use. For more information, please contact your local bookseller or the Hachette Book Group's Special Markets department at special.markets@hbgusa.com.

Printed in China

10 9 8 7 6 5 4 3 2 1

unionsquareandco.com

Editor: Amanda Englander
Designer: Laura Palese
Photographer: Johnny Miller
Food Stylist: Jess Damuck
Prop Stylist: Randi Brookman Harris
Art Director: Renée Bollier
Project Editor: Ivy McFadden
Production Manager: Terence Campo
Copy Editor: Terry Deal

Additional photo credits: Page 21: Molly DeCoudreaux

For Gus,
the life of my
party

My Kind of *Party*

WHEN MY FRIENDS ARE HEADING OUT FOR A ROWDY bachelorette weekend, a night at the club, or a crowded cocktail mixer, I tighten my robe and say, "You kids have fun!" as I wave them out the door. Hi, I'm Dan Pelosi, and my favorite kind of party is one where I can sit down. More specifically, I want to sit down to a delicious dinner, at an adorable table, surrounded by my fabulous friends and family. It's cozy, intimate, and my preferred way to celebrate. I have hosted countless parties like this in my life, and now, in my second cookbook, I want to tell you how I make every gathering feel like one I never want to leave. My absolute favorite part of hosting is sharing my corner of the world with the guests I invite in, and yes, that means you.

Here's my biggest secret (I know—can you believe I'm dropping it in the second paragraph?): Putting together a party doesn't have to be hard—and it shouldn't be. Just like riding a bike or learning to fold a fitted sheet, seamlessly weaving the act of gathering and celebrating into your day-to-day means you get to be present to appreciate the joy of bringing people together, feeling inspired by seasonal ingredients, and creating traditions that make any and every day feel special. Best of all, it means you can make any occasion feel like a party. You can be thoughtful and organized in such a way that your guests don't know this effortless event was, in reality, well planned—and that's what I want to help you do.

First let's take a quick stroll down memory lane. When I lived in San Francisco in my twenties, I found myself at lots of new kinds of "parties." I will never forget the night I met the world-famous drag queen Juanita MORE! at Booty Call, an event she hosted at a bar in the Castro District. In the middle of a DJ set, Juanita spotted me in the crowd, called me over to her booth, and handed me a homemade chocolate cupcake. Now *this* was my kind of party! We became instant friends, and soon I snagged an invite to her apartment for one of her famous dinner parties. I quickly became a regular guest at those dinner parties, and they are where much of my hosting education came from. My favorite detail was the menu Juanita would tack over her kitchen workstation before each event. It not only kept her on track as the hostess, it was also a fun preview of what was in store for us guests. Knowing she had taken the time and care to make a plan and write it out made these gatherings feel extra special.

Looking back, it's no surprise why Juanita's menu on the wall soothed me so deeply: because in my family, party planning—and just everyday meal planning—was synonymous with menu planning. While eating breakfast, we would plot what was for lunch. During lunch, we'd discuss dinner. And at dinner, we'd talk about what we were going to eat the next day. Obsessing over the perfect menu is in my DNA. Literally no one in my family has ever said yes to a party invite without knowing (or asking) exactly what would be on the menu first.

Given all that, it's probably no surprise to learn that when I'm planning a party, I start with the menu. And since I'm writing a book about parties, naturally it's organized entirely around menus. Any occasion—from the biggest soiree to the simplest dinner for two—wants, needs, and deserves a good menu. For me, that is and has always been the easiest way to host a successful gathering. It puts you at ease as the host, knowing your guests will be taken care of via the basics: food and drink. It allows you to use what you have on hand to create something special that sets the mood for the party. A good menu says, "Here's what to expect from this experience!" Plus, when your menu is set, all your guests have to worry about bringing are the good vibes.

The sixteen celebratory menus you'll find here take you through the year, embracing each season along the way. Some are big, some are small; some are expected, some are not. My very favorite party of the entire year is, of course, no surprise, but kind of a surprise, smack in the center of the book. No matter the theme, each menu celebrates the nostalgia of the parties of my past while also embracing all the new touches that are signature Grossy.

While each chapter was designed to be made as a whole menu, I hope that won't stop you from bringing your favorite individual recipes into regular weekday rotation, even when you're not *officially* partying. If you just happen to have a hankering for Caramelized Banana Pudding or Coconut Shrimp on a Tuesday night, I want you to have that. And if you want to have the baked beans from Let's Grill, Girls alongside the steak tips from Farmers' Market Feast, please do. Rest assured, you can adapt these menus and dishes to deliciousness any time of year, for any occasion, and turn them into your new staples. Easy to make and even easier to share, they'll help every hostess get her head in the game and cook up the kind of food guests will be talking about for weeks.

But hosting a party is about so much more than just putting food on the table: It's about creating an atmosphere where everyone feels welcome, relaxed, and ready to have a great time. Alongside the menus, you'll find tips on how to plan ahead so you can enjoy the party as much as your guests. There are ideas for staying on top of prep, setting the mood, and dealing with the aftermath, and lots of little tricks that make hosting seem effortless. The goal is to make every party a breeze, and I want you to be confident and excited about hosting, knowing that you have everything you need to create memorable experiences for your friends and family.

After years of throwing parties as my part-time job, I'm spilling everything I know about creating spaces that feel warm, spontaneous, and very satisfying. The heart of every great gathering is whom you share it with, and I firmly believe there's no greater pleasure than cooking for the people you love. My parties are never about perfection—rather, they're about making your guests feel welcome and having fun along the way. Whatever vibe you're going for, I hope this book inspires you to embrace the joy of coming together with good friends over great food. So please, take off your shoes (only if you want), find a comfy place to sit, grab a drink, and don't worry—the food will be served very soon.

LET'S GET THIS PARTY STARTED

I've spent a lot of time talking about what a Grossy party looks like, so now it's time to get the party started. Before you dive into this multicourse meal of a book, let me explain everything we're serving here.

A REASON TO PARTY Each of the parties in this book is inspired by a party I throw in my real life. Whether I'm grilling for the gays on Fire Island in the middle of summer or re-creating a steak house dinner at home for my girlfriends in the dead of winter, these are all my favorite ways to celebrate the everyday, every day.

ALL IN THE TIMING For each recipe, I've noted after the headnote if any components, or even the full recipe, can be made ahead—a real time-saver for weeknight cooking and entertaining alike. If you decide to go for it and tackle the full menu as I've outlined it, I've provided a timeline to ensure everything makes it onto the table when it should. My goal is to make your life easy, breezy, beautiful, and, most of all, delicious.

RECIPES I simply cannot say it enough: Before you do anything else, read from start to finish any recipe you plan to cook. Gus once learned the hard way, when company was due to arrive in a few hours, that a pie crust needed to rest overnight. I gently reminded him that there's no "win" in "winging it." Okay, maybe there is, but you get my point. Hosting is much less stressful when you feel confident in your plan, so get to know these recipes! As you plan, feel free to sub and swap ingredients to make these feel the most like you—and don't be shy about scribbling notes in the margins, while you're at it.

SERVING SIZES Serving sizes are always tricky to nail for a group because everyone has a different appetite, and how much they'll want of one dish all depends on what else is on the menu. If you're making one recipe by itself, keep in mind the serving sizes may shift when the table isn't loaded up with plenty of options to pass around. But if you're tackling a full menu, I can confidently say every recipe will serve 6 to 8 people— probably with leftovers to take home!— taking into account all the appetizers, sides, mains, or dessert alongside.

GROSSY GUIDES Throughout this book you'll find helpful guides filled with tips and tricks to help with successful party planning, hosting, or the simple things we all need for everyday cooking. In the spirit of hosting, I've invited over a few people to contribute guides as well. Whether you're just starting out or have years of experience, you should be having a fun fest, not a stress fest! These guides will ensure that your guests will return over and over again.

Now … Let's Party!

Grossy's Guide

THE BIG To-Dos

When you're planning a party, the guest list and grocery list need no introduction, but arguably the most important list is the to-do list. Instead of cramming all my chores into a couple of stressful days, I like to break them down into a checklist of easy-to-accomplish tasks leading up to the get-together. That way, instead of feeling a sense of impending doom, I'm building the party prep into the natural flow of my day-to-day. But not every party needs to be planned a month ahead, and sometimes you're just entertaining on a whim. That's where the beauty of this guide shines. Whether you've got weeks or a few hours, use this go-to checklist to keep things simple and stress-free.

Way Ahead

● **MAKE THE GUEST LIST**
My friend Juanita MORE! has some great advice for building the list on page 20.

● **SAVE THE DATE**
We all have hectic lives, so it's nice to get on everyone's calendar early.

● **PLAN THE MENU**
Choose dishes that feel exciting, using what's in season or on theme. Remember to ask your guests about any restrictions or allergies.

● **SHOP EARLY**
Get the pantry staples, like flour, sugar, and canned goods, crossed off the list now; it will be a big help later.

Week Of

- **CONFIRM THE GUEST LIST**
Send a reminder and finalize your head count.

- **LOCK THE MENU**
Make your full shopping list, planning when you'll shop for your most perishable items, and organize your prep and cooking schedule, assigning each task to a specific day.

- **DO A DEEP CLEAN**
My party-specific guide to cleaning on page 18 will help get you on the right track!

- **MAKE A SERVING PLAN**
Check that you have the tabletop essentials (see page 14). If you need anything special, pick it up now so you're not scrambling.

Day Before

- **SET UP THE SPACE**
Do final, quick clean; move any furniture; arrange seating; set the table (see page 14); make flower arrangements.

- **ORGANIZE YOUR DISHES**
Wash and dry the items you'll use to serve, and organize them in the kitchen so they're ready for plating as each dish is done.

- **COOK AWAY**
Don't save it all for tomorrow! Anything that can be made ahead should be made ahead. Most things taste better the next day anyway.

- **CHOOSE AN OUTFIT**
Pick out what you're going to wear and get it ready for its debut. Trust me, day of, you don't want to spend more time in the closet than you have to!

Last Minute

- **MAKE THE FINAL TOUCHES**
Light the (unscented) candles, start the playlist, and double-check you have everything you need so you can send out an SOS text now, before anyone arrives, if you need to.

- **TAKE OUT THE TRASH**
Be sure you're starting the party with empty, odor-free bins. Don't forget the bathroom trash, too.

- **GET DRESSED**
Pause all the other prep to put on your outfit, check your hair, and fix your lipstick. Your guests are about to arrive, and you don't want to be caught in your sports bra!

- **TAKE A DEEP BREATH**
You've got this. If there was ever a time to Live, Laugh, Love, it's right now.

Grossy's Guide

Setting the Table

I believe a beautifully set table is more about organization and less about stuff: Hosting is about having the *right* things, not *all* the things. So before you rush out to buy something new, let's get creative with what you already have.

I'm a big collector of objects (I'm a Taurus moon *and* rising, I can't help it) so when I'm thinking about my table, I most often think in themes and then find the objects that fit. What is the mood of the party? What colors are speaking to me right now? Did I just buy new glasses on vacation? Is now the time to put the adorable ceramic teddy bear salt and pepper shakers I bought on eBay seven years ago to use? (Yes.) Enjoy the process and don't be afraid to experiment! The most important thing you can bring to the table is your own sense of style. Here are my best tips, tricks, and reminders when it comes to setting the perfect scene.

Back to Basics

Ultimately, setting the table is about making sure everyone has what they need to enjoy their meal. Taking the time to get set means you also get to enjoy the meal without jumping up to run into the kitchen a million times. Basic table setting includes:

● TABLECLOTHS

To me, the difference between eating dinner and having a dinner party is a tablecloth. I probably should have mentioned that before page 14, but here we are. It's not required, obviously, but it *is* a special touch that makes your table feel like it's dressed up for an occasion. My mom would always let me pick the tablecloth for our family gatherings, and now Gus's mom helps me organize my fabulous collection of my own. When guests are coming, I am a kid again as I search to find the perfect one. While I have made table linens a big part of my party identity, you really only need one or two to have things covered (literally). And remember, the only difference between a tablecloth and a bedsheet is the name.

● PLACE MATS

If you can't bring yourself to buy a tablecloth after my fight song opposite, maybe I can interest you in place mats for under your plates? They are like little personal tablecloths for just *your* plate. I personally love to layer linens on linens—this is a real more is more situation for me—but again, place mats are not a necessity in any way.

● NAPKINS

I'm not above paper napkins, even if what's set out is actually a paper towel. But I do like to use cloth napkins for a touch of personality and sustainability when I have company. If you have talented seamstresses in your circle, you can ask them to sew 16 × 16-inch hemmed napkins using fabric you bought or found in your aunt's quilting closet (shout-out to Aunt Chris!). More than half my napkin collection was made this way! Napkins can either rest on the plate or under the fork. (I would never napkin ring, but don't let anyone yuck your yum!)

PLATES

A dinner plate is, quite literally, the center of the place setting. Most of the time, I keep it easy and stop right there. If you've craving something more formal, the bread plate goes above and to the left of the dinner plate, a salad plate rests on top of the dinner plate, and a soup bowl goes on top of the salad plate. Either way, be sure to clear all the plates before bringing out fresh ones for dessert.

FLATWARE

When you're laying down your flatware, remember the word *FORKS*. I know—it would be hard to forget—but what I mean is, working your way from left to right, *F* is for fork, *O* is the shape of your dinner plate, *R* makes this a cute acronym, *K* is for knife, and *S* is for spoon. I just set one fork, but if you wanted to use a salad fork that would go on the far left. Dinner knives should be set with the blade toward the plate and any smaller butter knives above the dinner plate, if you swing that way.

GLASSES

Personally, I tend to skip the nice glasses and instead stock up on two sizes of cheap glasses from Ikea or a restaurant supply store because A) breakage is inevitable when company comes (trust me, I have clumsy bear paws); and B) having plenty of glasses means you're free from cleaning duty during the party. I use my larger glasses for water and smaller glasses for fun drinks, like wine or cocktails. The water glass should go just above the knife and the fun glass to the right of it.

SERVEWARE

A good collection of platters and serving bowls is essential for successful hosting. But before you run out to Crate & Barrel, do a lap around your kitchen: Don't those mixing bowls look like serving bowls? Rimmed sheet pans make perfect platters. Add a clean kitchen towel to that colander to make a beautiful breadbasket. Cutting boards are happy to present everything from grilled meats to piled salads to a stack of sandwiches. That pasta pot was born to be an ice bucket or maybe a punch bowl. Even drinking glasses can come in handy for portioning out desserts!

SERVING UTENSILS

I often use my cooking utensils for serving. Tongs, wooden spoons, wide spatulas, and slotted spoons get the job done, so I don't worry about investing in specific, single-use tools, and you shouldn't either.

WATER

Every time I go to my best friend Tom's house, he proudly offers me a glass of his famous ice water (the recipe is—wait for it—ice and water). The joke literally never gets old, and he's not wrong: you can never have enough water at a party. Tap, filtered, sparkling . . . just make sure it's easy to access and there's plenty of it. If the meal is sit-down, a few pitchers on the table will help keep everyone hydrated without interrupting the conversation. As the host, you'll want to keep an eye on them to keep them full.

CORKSCREW WITH BOTTLE OPENER

It doesn't need to be on the table, but you do need to know exactly where it is. Get the rustling-through-drawers routine out of the way before your company arrives and find it a comfy home where it will stay visible to everyone.

Finishing Touches

Once the places are set, I like to add a few decorative elements to bring the table to life:

● CANDLES

If the sun is going down, I'm lighting candles. They don't have to be the only light in the room, but they never fail to add a magical glow. I love tall taper candles (especially if they're dripless) or short votives. But big or small, I believe in three important rules:

1. No scented candles. Your guests are there to enjoy the delicious food. Don't confuse them by burning Clean Cotton right under their noses.

2. If your candles are more than halfway used, replace them with new ones. A midmeal burnout is a bit of a mood killer.

3. Do a reach test: Sit in a few different seats, reach across the table, then set down your candles accordingly. When it's going to be a full house, I place the candles on a separate piece of furniture nearby so we can still enjoy the glow without going up in flames.

● FLOWERS

Flowers are always a gorgeous addition to the table, no matter the occasion. If a guest brings me a bouquet, I'll arrange it in a vase and set it somewhere near the table so we can admire the flowers without blocking anyone's view. Instead of one large centerpiece, I like to make several small, low arrangements so everyone can talk without having to crane their necks. For the table, I round up small vases, or a few small jars or glasses to scatter across the center. If flowers aren't in the budget, bowls of produce like citrus, stone fruit, tomatoes, squash, or bundles of herbs make for a beautiful centerpiece.

For the flowers themselves, I am the queen of using a couple bundles from the grocery. Here's how:

1. I prefer to buy bouquets of two or three types of flowers in a variety of shapes and colors. If the flowers are already in a mixed bouquet, separate them by type.

2. Working with one vessel at a time, choose a mix of flowers that look nice together. Odd numbers, like three or five, are more visually appealing. I don't make the rules!

3. Trim the stems enough so the flowers will hover a few inches above the rim of their vessel, varying the heights so each flower can have her own moment. Strip off any leaves that will fall below the waterline.

● MEET YOUR MISMATCH

I'm all for matching place settings, but I never feel drawn to them. To me, a mismatched table is a unique reflection of the host: If it looks great to you, your guests will love it too. My guests will often pick their seat based on the plate or napkin they love the most. Anchoring objects like matching plates and flatware gives you permission to add individuality in mismatched napkins and glasses. Or vice versa. Or mix and match the entire table. You decide!

THE GUEST-READY Glow-Up

Grossy's Guide

If you were here for my first book, *Let's Eat*, you'll remember how my mom upstaged me with her guide to deep cleaning the kitchen. (If you weren't, Jackie Pelosi alone makes it worth the price of admission.) Now it's *my* time to shine—literally and figuratively! The thing about guests is that you have to clean up before them and then you have to clean up after them, and, if you're me, you can even clean up *during* them! Here's my guide to all of it.

Before

● GET READY FOR YOUR CLOSE-UP

Deep clean all the common areas like the living room, dining room, kitchen, bathroom, entryway, and backyard. If coats are going on the bed (when and why did that become a universal thing?), be sure that room is clean, too. And if you're like me and a full house tour is simply mandatory upon entry, just go ahead and clean everything.

● MAKE THE TABLE SHINE

Be sure all tablecloths, napkins, glasses, plates, flatware, serving vessels, and utensils are presentable. A run through the laundry and dishwasher is good enough—no need to break out the polish and rags. But when you're done, be sure the washing machine, dishwasher, sink, and dish rack are emptied out so you can start the party with a clean slate.

● GIVE THE TRASH BINS A GOOD SCRUB

I would bet your trash and recycling (including the bathroom trash!) have been begging for some hot soapy water for a while. Now is the time to start fresh so no funky smells interrupt your party. Be sure bins are in obvious and accessible places. Remember to empty the bins after you prep, and pop in fresh bags right before your company arrives.

● STOCK UP ON PAPER GOODS

You're going to want to have plenty of paper towels handy to clean up spills. Set an extra roll or two of toilet paper in an obvious place in the bathroom—you don't want guest rifling through your cabinets!

● DON'T NEGLECT THE BATHROOM

It's likely everyone will be in there at some point. While you're stocking paper, tackle the trash can, refill the soap dispenser, and be sure to set out clean hand towels or a stack of paper napkins next to the sink.

During

● TIDY ALONG THE WAY

If the trash or recycling need to be emptied, do it, and swap in a new bag. Do a casual lap with a towel to wipe up any small spills or crumbs. Grab empty dishes and glasses and get them to the kitchen. This all helps keep the space clear and make the party feel less hectic and cluttered. Just make sure you're not pulling away from the party for too long—after a few minutes, you'll suddenly have a team of wannabe helpers following you around.

● STACK, BUT DON'T WASH

As items return to the kitchen from the party, swipe any trash into the bin and dump ice and liquids in the sink. Everyone loves leaving a dinner party with tomorrow's lunch in their purse, so I always make sure I have plenty of to-go containers at the ready for leftovers. Then start making a tidy stack of dirty plates, flatware, and glasses. Try to keep your sink empty so clean up is fast and easy later. Even if you're planning to load the dishwasher, save it for later. Much like disappearing for too long, obvious cleaning makes guests feel like they need to help and interrupts the party. One exception, though . . .

● TACKLE SPILLS IMMEDIATELY

Is it even a party if something doesn't spill? Don't panic; prepare. If you're sensitive about your furniture and carpets, avoid serving dark liquids. If you're more relaxed about it, keep a bottle of OxiClean or Wine Away on hand. And if you are caught unprepared despite my warnings, dig through your pantry for the old club soda and salt trick: Pour a healthy amount of salt on the stain, splash with a little club soda, let it sit for a few minutes, then blot with a kitchen towel. Repeat as needed until the stain lifts. Just don't be dramatic—guests will follow your lead.

● CALL IT A NIGHT

When you're ready for the party to be over, nicely tell everyone to leave. My go-to announcement is, "This has been SO fun, but it's approaching my bedtime." Most people will be relieved and ready to make their exit. The "party never ends" crowd will keep it going somewhere else—they don't have to go home, they just can't stay here, as they say.

After

● DELEGATE JOBS

There will always be a friend or two who offers to stay and help clean up. If you feel comfortable, say yes! And if there are any partners or children hanging around, get them up and moving, too. Many hands make light work, so don't take it all on yourself.

● RESIST THE URGE TO SIT DOWN

While you're still up on your feet, get all those dishes into the dishwasher. Soak anything that needs it. Wipe down the main surfaces. Throw the linens in the washing machine. Grab the vacuum or at least the dust buster for a quick once-over. Take out the trash. Save the deep clean for tomorrow when you have more energy, but get started tonight so you don't feel like you're waking up in a frat house.

● RECLAIM YOUR SPACE

Open the windows to air out the space. Slide the furniture back so you don't stub your toe in the middle of the night. Fluff the pillows and fold the blankets. Grab a scented candle, incense, or room spray. Start making it feel like your space again.

● TAKE NOTES

Once you do sit down, grab a pen and paper (or this book!). Jot down what worked and what didn't, what was a hit and what was a miss. Scribble any notes about specific recipes while they're still fresh in your mind. The next time you have people over, you'll be glad for these reminders.

JUANITA MORE!'s *Guide*
THE *Guest List*

My friend, the world-famous San Francisco drag queen Juanita MORE!, knows a thing or two about guest lists. Hers are always the most sought-after in town—whether at the club or around her own table. She taught me so much about how to entertain flawlessly, most especially getting the right group gathered for a meal. She has a special way of inviting an eclectic mix of people into her (night)life and her home. I asked her to share her top three tips for building the perfect guest list, and here's what she had to say:

HOW TO
Curate the List

To guarantee a fabulous guest list for dinner, I first love to invite the die-hard foodies who will eat anything I prepare. I also try to create a good mix of personalities and people from different parts of my life—all of that is in hopes of growing new friendships. Then, I always save a seat for someone who likes to gossip, which makes the dinner conversation sparkle . . . for obvious reasons. I welcome all without judgment, preconditions, or expectations. I consider everyone royalty when they dine at my place.

HOW TO
Get Everyone Mingling

Connecting people is one of my specialties, and I have a long history of welcoming newcomers into my circle. I often find the universe has put us in the same room for a reason, and we all share something. So I listen to everyone's story, and if it reminds me of someone else's in the room, I'll make that introduction. I always have a secret seating plan, and I put guests next to each other for conversation or to help me in the kitchen. There is always someone at the table who was once a server, so they sit next to me. I enjoy watching them stack plates up their arms to place in front of guests at the table. I pass the wine bottle to the shy person, allowing them to interact with all the guests as they pour.

HOW TO
NOT Get Invited Back

You'll always be invited back unless you're a bad guest. Tardiness is something I am most annoyed about. I have had to remind a few people running late that "I am not reheating a frozen pizza over here!" Someone once arrived late with a half-eaten box of Thai food in their hands. I asked why they were carrying a take-out box, and they replied they got hungry on the way over. Like, what? I still shake my head about that one. But, most notably, just like my dislike for floral bouquets (I only have a certain number of vases and they will be filled with arrangements already!), please do not bring a surprise plus one. That's the fastest way to get crossed off my list.

The *P*

rties

Farmers' Market *Feast*

Make THE Menu

● **2 DAYS BEFORE**

Farmers' Market Salad with Avocado Ranch: Make the avocado ranch dressing and store in the fridge.

Smashed Pickled Cucumber Salad: Prepare the cucumbers and radishes, add the brine, and store in the fridge.

Cath's String Bean & Potato Pasta: Make the pesto and store in the fridge.

Marinated Steak Tips over Herby Rice: Marinate the steak tips and store in the fridge.

Roasted Fig & Goat Cheese Parfaits: Roast the figs and store in the fridge.

● **1 DAY BEFORE**

Melted Leek & Lemon Roast Chicken: Spatchcock the chicken, season it, and marinate in the fridge.

Marinated Steak Tips over Herby Rice: Prepare the herby rice and store in the fridge.

Roasted Fig & Goat Cheese Parfaits: Assemble the parfaits and store in the fridge.

I DIDN'T GROW UP GOING TO FARMERS' MARKETS.

My earliest food memories are a mix of ShopRite runs and digging through Bimpy's backyard garden. It wasn't until I studied abroad in Rome during college that I discovered their magic.

I was hypnotized by Campo de' Fiori, the bustling Roman market loaded with vibrant produce, accompanied by the hectic shouts of vendors. I became a regular, weaving through the stalls and exploring new flavors. It opened me up to a whole new world of cooking.

I have sought out—and found—a piece of that Roman charm in every city I've lived in thereafter. In San Francisco, the Ferry Plaza Farmers Market was my second home. In New York, the Union Square Greenmarket became part of my routine. When I'm at my house upstate, the Copake Hillsdale Famers Market is unmissable. Wherever I go, the local market keeps me connected to the seasons and the people who grow our food. Grab your reusable bags, girls: It's time to hit the market!

● **MORNING OF**

Farmers' Market Salad with Avocado Ranch: Chop the vegetables for the salad and store in the fridge.

● **ONE HOUR BEFORE**

Cath's String Bean & Potato Pasta: Cook the pasta and veggies and toss with the pesto.

Melted Leek & Lemon Roast Chicken: Preheat the grill or oven and roast the chicken, basting every 15 minutes.

Marinated Steak Tips over Herby Rice: Reheat the rice.

● **30 MINUTES BEFORE**

Farmers' Market Salad with Avocado Ranch: Combine the kale and cabbage with the dressing, massage, and let rest.

Smashed Pickled Cucumber Salad: Drain the brine and garnish with fresh dill and black pepper.

Marinated Steak Tips over Herby Rice: Grill the steak and arrange over the rice.

● **SERVING TIME**

Farmers' Market Salad with Avocado Ranch: Add the chopped vegetables to the salad.

Melted Leek & Lemon Roast Chicken: Carve the chicken and arrange in the skillet.

Roasted Fig & Goat Cheese Parfaits: Serve the parfaits straight from the fridge for dessert.

Farmers' Market Salad *with* Avocado Ranch

Serves 6 to 8

This salad is a celebration of how beautiful fresh veggies can be. Too often, I improvise a salad from whatever's about to die in my fridge. But there's a special delight in walking through the market, selecting the freshest, prettiest produce, and building a bowl with purpose. The crunch! The flavor explosion! Oh, and the creamy avocado ranch dressing doesn't hurt, either. Mom always said to eat the rainbow, and this salad is a delicious reminder to do just that!

Make Ahead: The dressing can be refrigerated in an airtight container up to 3 days.

AVOCADO RANCH

I cup mayonnaise

½ cup buttermilk

I tablespoon white wine vinegar

I teaspoon onion powder

½ teaspoon garlic powder

¼ teaspoon kosher salt, plus more as needed

¼ teaspoon freshly ground black pepper, plus more as needed

I avocado, halved, pitted, and peeled

¼ cup loosely packed fresh parsley leaves

¼ cup loosely packed fresh dill

I bunch chives

SALAD

I bunch lacinato kale, woody stems discarded and leaves roughly torn

½ head purple cabbage, cored and diced

I ear corn, shucked and kernels removed

I large red bell pepper, diced

I large carrot, chopped

I. MAKE THE AVOCADO RANCH: In a blender or food processor, combine the mayonnaise, buttermilk, vinegar, onion powder, garlic powder, salt, and pepper. Blend on medium speed until combined, about 30 seconds. Scrape down the sides and add the avocado, parsley, dill, and chives. Blend for about 30 seconds more to make a smooth dressing. Taste for seasoning and add more salt and pepper as needed.

2. MAKE THE SALAD: In a large bowl, combine the kale, cabbage, and I cup of the dressing. Use your hands to massage and thoroughly coat the ingredients. Add another spoonful or two of dressing as desired. Set aside to rest for about 30 minutes.

3. Sprinkle the corn, bell pepper, and carrot over the top of the kale and cabbage. Serve with the remaining dressing in a small bowl on the side for drizzling.

Smashed Pickled Cucumber Salad

Serves 6 to 8

When Gus and I started dating, he had a job waiting tables at a restaurant—I'd occasionally stop by just to bat my eyes at him and, obviously, have a snack. They had these incredible house-made bread and butter pickles on the menu that I would plunge my fork into and eat like a salad. I wanted to replicate that joy with this pickle-inspired salad. Chunky bites of smashed cucumbers plus the spicy bite of crunchy radishes have a soak in a garlicky brine. They're ready the next day, but like any worthy batch of pickles, a nice long soak only improves the flavor.

Make Ahead: The veggies can be refrigerated in their brine up to 1 month.

8 radishes, trimmed and quartered

2 pounds mini cucumbers

¼ cup sugar

2 tablespoons coarsely chopped fresh dill, plus more for serving

2 garlic cloves, thinly sliced

1 tablespoon kosher salt

Red pepper flakes (optional)

2 cups distilled white vinegar, plus more as needed

Freshly ground black pepper

1. Place the radishes in a clean 2-quart jar or airtight container. Use the flat side of a knife to lightly smash the cucumbers, then roughly chop them. Add them to the jar along with the sugar, dill, garlic, salt, and a pinch of pepper flakes (if using).

2. Pour the vinegar into the jar. Screw on the lid and shake until the sugar and salt dissolve. Fill the jar to the brim with more vinegar as needed, then tighten the lid and refrigerate for at least 24 hours or up to 1 month.

3. Drain the brine and arrange the pickled salad in a serving bowl. Finish with a little bit of dill and a few grinds of black pepper before serving.

Cath's String Bean & Potato Pasta

Serves 6 to 8

This dish is a specialty of Gus's mom, Cath, and it's her go-to for getting something on the table when she suddenly has a crowd to feed, which happens often when I am visiting. (I find friends everywhere I go; what can I say?) When I finally asked her for the recipe, I was shocked by how easy it is to make! It's essentially a one-pot meal, since the potatoes, pasta, and green beans all boil together in the same water. You can use a jar of store-bought pesto to really streamline this on a busy night, but it's nice to take a couple extra minutes to make my own fresh batch. Cath never makes the same pesto twice, throwing in any mix of leafy greens and swapping around different seeds and nuts. I, too, am pesto-flexible, but for this dish I personally love a rich walnut-and-basil version. She serves this pasta warm for dinner, but it's equally delicious cold the next day.

Make Ahead: The pesto can be refrigerated in an airtight container up to 3 days. The vegetables and pasta can be assembled and refrigerated overnight.

Kosher salt

1 pound dried gemelli pasta

1 pound new potatoes, scrubbed and halved

½ pound green beans, trimmed and cut into 1-inch pieces

½ cup raw walnuts

½ cup freshly grated Parmesan cheese

2 garlic cloves

2 cups packed fresh basil leaves, plus more for serving

Zest and juice of 1 lemon

1 cup extra-virgin olive oil

Freshly ground black pepper

1. Bring a large pot of salted water to a boil over high heat. Add the pasta and potatoes. Cook until the pasta is al dente according to the package directions and the potatoes are fork-tender, adding the green beans 1 minute before the pasta is done. Reserve 1 cup of the cooking water, then drain.

2. Meanwhile, in a food processor, combine the walnuts, Parmesan, garlic, and 1 teaspoon salt. Process until the walnuts are finely chopped, about 1 minute. Scrape down the sides and add the basil, lemon zest, and lemon juice. Pulse about 4 times until the basil is roughly chopped. Scrape the mixture into a large bowl and whisk in the olive oil.

3. Add the pasta, potatoes, and green beans to the bowl with the pesto. Add about ¼ cup of the reserved cooking water and use a spatula to fold until everything is thoroughly coated. Add another splash or two of cooking water as needed to reach your desired consistency.

4. Serve hot, let cool to room temperature, or refrigerate overnight. Garnish with whole basil leaves and plenty of pepper before serving.

Melted Leek & Lemon Roast Chicken

Serves 6 to 8

Spatchcocking a chicken—removing the spine and laying it flat—helps with even cooking, rendering juicy meat and crispy skin across the entire bird. In this slow-roasted dish, the leek and lemon melt into the sauce and the outside of the bird gets brown and beautiful. The key here is consistent basting so the meat stays moist and the skin gets blanketed in the fat pooling below. The reward after all that work is a deeply flavored skillet sauce that almost steals the show. I guarantee this will immediately become one of your go-to chicken recipes, deserving of its own party!

Make Ahead: The chicken can marinate up to 24 hours.

1 (4-pound) whole chicken

2 tablespoons sugar

1 tablespoon kosher salt

3 lemons

1 large or 2 small leeks, halved lengthwise, rinsed well, and cut into 2-inch pieces

2 tablespoons extra-virgin olive oil

Freshly ground black pepper

½ to 1 cup low-sodium chicken broth

1. Place the chicken on a cutting board so the breast side is down and the drumsticks are facing you. Find the spine running down the center of the chicken. Use kitchen shears to cut along either side of the spine and remove it. Flip the chicken breast side up and spread out the edges. Press hard in the center of the breastplate to snap it so the chicken lies flat. Pat the chicken dry all over with paper towels.

2. In a small bowl, combine the sugar, salt, and the zest of 2 of the lemons. Pinch the mixture with your fingers until a thick paste forms. Spread half the paste over the inside of the chicken, rubbing to evenly distribute it over the meat. Rub the rest of the mixture evenly over the skin side of the chicken. Line a large plate with paper towels and set the chicken on top. Marinate in the fridge, uncovered, for at least 4 hours or up to 48 hours.

3. Preheat the oven to 400°F.

4. Arrange the leeks evenly over the bottom of a large cast-iron skillet. Thinly slice the remaining 1 lemon and arrange the pieces in the skillet. Cut the two zested lemons in half and squeeze the juice directly into the skillet. Add the olive oil. Cook over medium heat, stirring occasionally, until the leeks start to soften, about 10 minutes. Remove from the heat.

5. Transfer the chicken straight from the fridge to the top of the leeks and lemons, skin side up. Blanket the skin with pepper.

6. Place the skillet in the oven and roast the chicken for 1 hour, stopping every 15 minutes to spoon the juices over the skin. After the first basting, add ½ cup of the chicken broth to the bottom of the skillet. After the third basting, if needed, add another ½ cup if the skillet looks dry.

7. Remove the skillet from the oven and baste one more time. Let the chicken rest for 15 minutes, then transfer to a carving board. Slice to remove the thighs, then cut between the thighs and drumsticks to break into separate sections. Cut down the center of the breastbone along the ribs to release each breast, then cut each one across in half to make four pieces. Nestle all the chicken pieces back in the skillet around the lemon and leek pieces.

8. Serve family-style with a large spoon for scooping chicken pieces, leeks, lemons, and pan sauce.

Note

To make this recipe on the grill, prepare the grill for medium heat, about 400°F (see page 65). Arrange everything in the skillet without cooking, set the chicken on top, and blanket with pepper. Set on the grill grates over direct heat and close the lid. Follow the same instructions for baking and basting.

Marinated Steak Tips *over* Herby Rice

Serves 6 to 8

Ninety Nine Restaurant & Pub is a chain in New England that's famous for steak tips. They're perfectly marinated, nicely charred, and served over buttery, herby rice. The dish is absolute perfection, especially for a family-style feast. Steak tips are a popular New England cut, but it's just sirloin or tenderloin sliced into cubes. Even though the rice and steak cook quickly, it's worth planning to make this one a couple days ahead because the longer the steak marinates, the more tender and flavorful it'll be, saturating the soft rice with its incredible juices.

Make Ahead: The rice can be refrigerated in an airtight container up to 3 days; reheat in a large saucepan over low heat with a splash of water. The steak tips can marinate up to 48 hours.

STEAK TIPS

3 pounds steak tips or sirloin steak, cut into 1-inch pieces

1 large red onion, chopped

3 tablespoons extra-virgin olive oil

2 tablespoons Worcestershire sauce or soy sauce

1 teaspoon kosher salt

1 teaspoon freshly ground black pepper

1 teaspoon garlic powder

1 teaspoon onion powder

½ teaspoon red pepper flakes

10 thyme sprigs

4 rosemary sprigs

4 parsley sprigs

1 lemon, halved

HERBY RICE

2 cups long-grain white rice, rinsed

¾ cup (1½ sticks) unsalted butter

½ teaspoon kosher salt

2 tablespoons fresh thyme leaves

2 tablespoons chopped fresh rosemary leaves

2 tablespoons chopped fresh parsley

Neutral oil, for greasing

1. MAKE THE STEAK TIPS: In a large zip-top bag or airtight container, combine the steak, onion, olive oil, Worcestershire, salt, black pepper, garlic powder, onion powder, and pepper flakes. Seal the bag and smoosh everything around until the steak is well coated. Add the herbs to the bag, seal, and smoosh again. Marinate in the fridge for at least 8 hours or up to 48 hours.

2. MAKE THE HERBY RICE: In a large saucepan, combine the rice and 3 cups water. Set over high heat to bring to a boil. Stir the rice well, cover, and reduce the heat to low. Simmer until the liquid is mostly absorbed and the rice is cooked through, about 15 minutes. Remove from the heat and let rest, still covered, for about 5 minutes. Add the butter and salt and stir until the butter is melted. Add the herbs and stir again. Cover to keep warm.

3. Prepare the grill for high heat and lightly grease the grates with neutral oil (see page 65).

4. Remove the steak from the marinade and allow the excess to drip off. Thread the steak and onions onto separate skewers, until mostly full. Arrange the skewers on the grill. Close the lid and cook for about 5 minutes, until the bottoms of the skewers are nicely charred. Flip the skewers, cover again, and cook for another 5 minutes, until charred on the other side.

5. Spread out the rice on a serving platter. Place the grilled skewers on top of the rice and let rest for about 10 minutes, lightly tenting with foil to keep warm.

6. Meanwhile, set the lemon halves, cut side down, on the grill and cook until the bottoms are nicely charred, about 4 minutes, then arrange on the side of the rice. Squeeze the grilled lemon over the skewers and rice just before serving.

Note

To make this recipe on the stove, use a preheated large cast-iron skillet over medium-high heat, coated with 1 tablespoon of neutral oil.

Roasted Fig & Goat Cheese Parfaits

Serves 8

Figs were a big part of my childhood. There were stacks of dried or fresh figs on the table after meals, packets of Fig Newtons in my mom's purse for snacking, fig-filled cuccidati cookies at Christmas . . . it's one of those flavors that immediately makes me feel like a kid again. This recipe makes them more grown-up by roasting them with fresh rosemary for an herbal touch, then layering them into a parfait with a tart goat cheese whipped cream and buttery shortbread cookie crumbs. I especially love this dessert when I'm hosting, since it can be assembled as individual servings and refrigerated long before company arrives.

Make Ahead: The parfaits can be refrigerated up to 24 hours.

I pound fresh figs, trimmed and halved lengthwise

Kosher salt

Honey

3 tablespoons finely chopped fresh rosemary

I (10-ounce) box shortbread cookies, such as Lorna Doone

4 tablespoons (½ stick) unsalted butter

8 ounces goat cheese

¾ cup heavy cream, very cold

3 tablespoons sugar

I. Preheat the oven to 400°F. Line a rimmed sheet pan with foil.

2. Arrange the figs, cut side up, on the prepared sheet pan. Season with a pinch of salt and drizzle generously with honey, then sprinkle the rosemary on top. Bake for about 15 minutes, until the figs are tender but not falling apart. Let cool.

3. Meanwhile, place the cookies in a zip-top bag and use a rolling pin (or your hands!) to smash into fine crumbs. Melt the butter in a large skillet over medium heat. Add the crumbs to the butter along with a pinch of salt and a generous drizzle of honey and stir to combine everything. Cook, stirring often, until the crumbs are golden and fragrant, about 3 minutes. Transfer the crumbs to a medium bowl to cool.

4. In a medium bowl, combine the goat cheese and heavy cream. Using a handheld mixer on low, whip the two together. Add the sugar. Increase the speed to medium and whip until light and fluffy, about 2 minutes.

5. Spoon about 2 tablespoons of the cream mixture into each of 8 small (8-ounce) jars or glasses. Sprinkle a thick layer of crumbs, about 2 tablespoons each, over top, then layer on 2 or 3 figs. Repeat for a second layer, ending with the figs. Seal the jars or cover with cling wrap. Refrigerate until ready to serve.

Grossy's Guide

SHOPPING THE

Farmers' Market

Farmers' markets are where I go to get my fill of all the best local produce, meats, and cheeses (and maybe a little local gossip, too). Local farmers' markets are the most sustainable way to shop, as the produce doesn't have to travel too far, and neither do I. A self-proclaimed queen of the farmers' market, I am ready to share everything I know about ascending the throne.

Ready, Set …

Before heading out the door, make sure you have the essentials:

REUSABLE BAGS: Bring a few big, sturdy tote bags to carry your haul. I always keep a couple in my car so they're on hand when I need them. Smaller cloth bags are also a good idea for separating produce, or you can give any old plastic bags, like old newspaper bags, zip-top bags, or grocery bags, a second life here. If you're planning to shop for meat, fish, or dairy, an insulated bag or cooler with ice packs is smart.

CASH: Many vendors will have an option to tap or transfer, but having cash, especially small bills, can help make transactions smoother and keeps your farmers from getting hit with processing fees. It's a nice gesture that goes a long way.

SHOPPING LIST: Unlike a grocery store, the supply at a farmers' market will vary from week to week, but you should still come with a loose plan so you don't feel overwhelmed. Know what you're looking for generally, but be open to substitution and spontaneity.

All in the Timing

If you're a serious market shopper, you're either an early bird or a latecomer. I'm team early bird, but both have serious advantages:

EARLY BIRDS: Arriving right when the market opens gives you the first pick of the produce. Popular or hyper-seasonal items can sell out quickly, so being first in line ensures the best selection.

LATECOMERS: If you're looking for deals, swing by just before closing. Vendors often start discounting unsold produce to lighten the load back to the farm. The selection may be more limited, but the prices are unbeatable.

Personable Shopper

The best part of a farmers' market is getting to meet the people who grow your food. Take advantage of all that firsthand knowledge!

ASK QUESTIONS: Farmers know their produce better than anyone, so pick their brains for everything from proper storage to simple recipe recommendations. So much of my education around food has come from these kinds of interactions.

TAKE A BITE: Many vendors will let you sample a berry or rip off a leaf to take a taste. (Always ask first!) There will probably be fruits, vegetables, herbs, and greens you've never heard of, so explore your options!

BUILD RELATIONSHIPS: If you love a vendor's produce, let them know— and keep coming back for more. Loyalty is rewarded over time with special deals, secret stashes, and sneak peeks. And if you know you're going to need 12 pounds of apples to make pies for multiple Thanksgiving stops, now you know who to ask.

Waste Not

The whole point of the farmers' market is sustainability, and a big part of that falls on your shoulders as the buyer. Here are the best ways to be sure you're a smart shopper, not a wasteful one:

PLAN IT OUT: Having a rough—and realistic—idea of meals for the week will help keep you on track when shopping. It's great to have a fridge stuffed with fresh produce, but it doesn't help anyone if you don't use it.

BULKING UP: Sometimes buying produce in bulk is a great way to cut your grocery bill. If you have the time, energy, and space to freeze or preserve fresh produce for later in the year, go for it!

OPEN SEASON: The US is a huge country, so seasonality shifts depending on where you live. Your farmers will be the best authority on when specific produce is available in your area, so trust their advice over any online guides. The peak season stuff is always worth waiting for.

BRING IT BACK: Most farmers' markets will have a collection for organic waste that will be turned into compost. Throughout the week, save scraps, coffee grounds, and eggshells in an airtight container. If anything is dying in the crisper drawer, bring that with you, too. All that food waste will skip the landfill and be reused to grow new produce.

Let's Grill, *Girls!*

Make THE Menu

● 2 DAYS BEFORE

Tomato & Fennel Baked Beans: Make the baked beans and store in the fridge.

Balsamic Barbecued Ribs: Bake and cool the ribs and make the sauce. Store separately in the fridge.

● 1 DAY BEFORE

Dad's Grilled Swordfish with Pickled Salsa: Marinate the swordfish and make the pickled salsa. Store separately in the fridge.

Grossy P's Arnie P: Make the lemonade and iced tea. Store separately in the fridge.

FOR YEARS, APARTMENT LIVING FOR ME MEANT

cooking in tiny kitchens. Any time my friends and I would rent a vacation house—always with a patio and grill, of course—my inner grill girl would come alive: glowing (read: sweaty) and smiling. There's nothing like piling ingredients onto a bunch of sheet pans, then lining them all up to have their turn on the grates. The grill brings you outside the kitchen, letting you soak up the sun and hang out with your friends while you cook. Plus, the grill is in the biggest kitchen I know of—the great outdoors!

Now that I have a house in the country, I'm living my grill girl fantasy full-time (and not just because my kitchen was under renovation for eight months!). Grilling isn't just about making great food; it's an experience. The sizzle of the meat, the aroma wafting through the air, the feeling of flipping veggies while the sun sets. Every time I ignite my grill, I'm transported to a place of pure joy where worries melt away with each turn of the tongs.

Burgers and dogs are obvious. But this chapter goes beyond all that because I'm convinced pretty much everything can be made over the grates. Fire up and let's grill, girls!

● **1 HOUR BEFORE**

Garlic Bread Grilled Corn: Toast the panko and season.

Grilled Zucchini Caprese: Grill the zucchini and assemble the salad.

Tomato & Fennel Baked Beans: Reheat the baked beans and keep warm.

● **30 MINUTES BEFORE**

Garlic Bread Grilled Corn: Grill the corn and coat.

Balsamic Barbecued Ribs: Heat the barbecue sauce, slather the ribs, and grill.

Dad's Grilled Swordfish with Pickled Salsa: Grill the swordfish and top with the salsa.

● **SERVING TIME**

Grossy P's Arnie P: Set out lemonade, iced tea, and garnishes.

Grilled Pound Cake & Peaches: Grill the pound cake and peaches for dessert.

Garlic Bread Grilled Corn

Serves 6 to 8

There are a million ways to grill corn, but I'm all about that char, so I like to toss my cobs straight onto the grill grates until they're blazing yellow and deeply blackened. You could stop there and just slather on some butter, but why would you do that? Inspired by my love for all things garlic bread, I coat these charred beauties in mayonnaise (what can't she do?!) and roll them through crispy, garlicky, heavily seasoned breadcrumbs. Light, easy, and irresistibly delicious, this is my dream summer cob.

I cup panko breadcrumbs

4 garlic cloves, grated

I teaspoon Italian seasoning

I teaspoon kosher salt

½ teaspoon freshly ground black pepper

¼ teaspoon red pepper flakes

¼ teaspoon smoked paprika

½ cup freshly grated Parmesan cheese

Neutral oil, for greasing

6 ears of corn, shucked and halved crosswise

4 tablespoons (½ stick) unsalted butter, melted

½ cup mayonnaise

1. In a medium skillet, combine the panko and garlic and spread the mixture in an even layer. Cook over low heat, stirring constantly as the panko toasts, until golden brown, about 8 minutes. Remove from the heat and immediately stir in the Italian seasoning, salt, black pepper, pepper flakes, and paprika. Let the mixture cool for 5 minutes, then stir in the Parmesan.

2. Prepare the grill for high heat and lightly grease the grates with neutral oil (see page 65).

3. Head to the grill with the corn, melted butter, mayonnaise, and skillet of breadcrumbs. Generously brush each cob all over with melted butter and place on the grill. Close the lid and cook until nicely charred on the bottom, 4 to 5 minutes. Flip, then cover and grill until charred on the other side, about 5 minutes more. Transfer to a serving platter and let rest until cool enough to handle.

4. Holding one cob vertically, slather a layer of mayonnaise all around the corn. Immediately roll the cob through the seasoned breadcrumbs, pressing to adhere, and return it to the platter. Repeat with the remaining cobs, then serve.

Note

To make this recipe on the stove, lightly brush a preheated large skillet or grill pan with neutral oil and set over high heat.

Grilled Zucchini Caprese

Serves 6 to 8

Here's the beauty of this dish: It can be served hot off the grill *or* made ahead of time and chilled for later. When it comes to entertaining, heteroflexible recipes are just my type. Fresh summer zucchini has a subtle sweetness that fits right in with the flavors of a classic caprese, tucked between juicy tomatoes, fragrant basil, and creamy mozzarella. The honey vinaigrette on top seals the deal. The combination is so good, you'll wonder why zucchini wasn't part of the original girl group!

Make Ahead The vinaigrette can be refrigerated in an airtight container up to 3 days. The caprese can be assembled, covered with cling wrap, and refrigerated up to 4 hours.

Neutral oil, for greasing

HONEY VINAIGRETTE

2 tablespoons white wine vinegar

2 tablespoons honey

1 tablespoon extra-virgin olive oil

½ teaspoon kosher salt

½ teaspoon freshly ground black pepper, plus more for serving

Pinch of red pepper flakes

CAPRESE

2 heirloom tomatoes, cut into ½-inch-thick slices

½ cup cherry tomatoes, halved

Flaky sea salt

2 medium zucchini, cut on a diagonal into ½-inch-thick pieces

Extra-virgin olive oil

1 pound fresh mozzarella cheese, cut into ½-inch-thick slices

Fresh basil leaves, for serving

1. Prepare the grill for high heat and lightly grease the grates with the neutral oil (see page 65).

2. **MAKE THE HONEY VINAIGRETTE:** In a small bowl, whisk together the vinegar, honey, olive oil, salt, black pepper, and pepper flakes.

3. **MAKE THE CAPRESE:** Season the tomato slices with a good pinch of flaky salt and set aside to get their juices flowing.

4. Generously drizzle the tops of the zucchini with olive oil, then lay the slices, oil side down, on the grill. Close the lid and cook until nicely charred on one side, about 5 minutes. Drizzle with more olive oil, then flip, cover, and cook until charred on the other side, about 5 minutes more. Transfer to a plate to cool slightly.

5. On a serving platter, shingle the zucchini, tomatoes, and mozzarella. Drape and tuck basil leaves all around the plate. Whisk the vinaigrette again and evenly pour it over the caprese. Finish with more black pepper and a little more flaky salt before serving.

Note

To make this recipe on the stove, use a preheated large skillet over medium heat, coated with ¼ cup of neutral oil. Cook the zucchini in batches for about 3 minutes on each side. Transfer to paper towels to drain while cooking the rest.

Tomato & Fennel Baked Beans

Serves 6 to 8

I grew up in New England, where baked beans were a staple of every backyard barbecue. Another staple of every backyard barbecue was my family showing up and letting you know we were Italian, primarily through our food. This version is my loudly, proudly Italian twist on the barbecue classic. This pot of beans is best made on the stove (or grill side burner) and reheated over the grill while everything else sizzles away. It starts with a base of crispy, salty pancetta, thinly sliced fennel, and diced tomatoes slowly melting together, plus a whole bottle of Peroni—summer in a pot! I like cannellini for a reliably creamy, sturdy bean that stands up to a simmer.

Make Ahead The beans can be made and refrigerated in an airtight container up to 3 days. Reheat gently in a large saucepan with a splash of water on the stove over low heat, or directly on the grill grates.

4 ounces pancetta, cubed

1 large fennel bulb, halved and thinly sliced, fronds reserved

Kosher salt

1 beefsteak tomato, diced

1 (12-ounce) bottle Peroni beer or any light lager

2 tablespoons dark brown sugar

2 tablespoons tomato paste

2 (15.5-ounce) cans cannellini beans, drained and rinsed

1. In a large saucepan, combine the pancetta with 2 tablespoons water and cook over medium-high heat, stirring occasionally, until the water evaporates and the pancetta browns, about 4 minutes.

2. Add the fennel and a pinch of salt. Cook, scraping up any browned bits from the bottom of the pan, until the fennel begins to soften and stick to the pan, about 6 minutes. Add the tomato and about half the beer. Stir well, cover, and simmer until the tomato and fennel are falling apart, about 5 minutes.

3. Stir in the brown sugar and tomato paste. Add the beans, the remaining beer, and another pinch of salt. Continue to simmer, uncovered, stirring occasionally, until the sauce has thickened, 5 to 7 minutes. Stir in the reserved fennel fronds just before serving straight from the pan.

Note
The beans can be reheated in the covered saucepan directly on the grill grates as you're grilling the rest of the menu.

Balsamic Barbecued Ribs

Serves 6 to 8

Everyone loves a burger and hot dog fresh off the grill, but a rack of saucy, tender ribs is my personal MVP. The key is to bake them low and slow in the oven until they're almost falling apart, let them cool so they firm back up, and then blanket them in barbecue sauce before quickly charring on the grill. By the time the sauce is caramelized, the ribs are barely hanging on to their bones! Bottled BBQ sauce is perfect (Sweet Baby Ray's girls unite!), but trust me, this homemade balsamic barbecue sauce is sweet, sassy, extra tangy, and absolutely worth it. Pass me a Wet-Nap?

Make Ahead The barbecue sauce can be refrigerated in an airtight container up to 2 weeks. The baked ribs can be wrapped in foil and refrigerated up to 3 days.

RIBS

¼ cup kosher salt

2 tablespoons freshly ground black pepper

2 tablespoons garlic powder

2 tablespoons onion powder

2 tablespoons ground mustard

2 tablespoons smoked paprika

8 pounds baby back ribs or St. Louis–style spareribs

BALSAMIC BARBECUE SAUCE

1 medium white onion, diced

4 garlic cloves, smashed

1 cup balsamic vinegar

½ cup ketchup

¼ cup packed dark brown sugar

¼ cup spicy brown mustard

2 tablespoons Worcestershire sauce

1 tablespoon smoked paprika

1 teaspoon kosher salt

½ teaspoon red pepper flakes

Neutral oil, for greasing

1. Center two oven racks, spacing them one rung apart, and preheat the oven to 300°F.

2. **MAKE THE RIBS:** In a small bowl, whisk together the salt, black pepper, garlic powder, onion powder, ground mustard, and paprika. Lay each rack of ribs on a double layer of foil. Season them on all sides with the spice rub, then wrap tightly. Place each bundle on a rimmed sheet pan and transfer to the oven. Bake for 2½ to 3 hours, until the ribs are extremely tender but not falling apart.

3. **MEANWHILE, MAKE THE SAUCE:** In a blender, combine the onion, garlic, balsamic vinegar, ketchup, brown sugar, mustard, Worcestershire, paprika, salt, and pepper flakes. Blend on high speed until smooth, scraping down the sides as needed, about 3 minutes. Pour the mixture into a large saucepan and set over high heat. Bring to a boil, then reduce the heat to low and cook, stirring occasionally, until glossy and reduced by about half, about 20 minutes.

4. Remove the ribs from the oven and open the top of each foil packet to let the hot steam escape. Transfer to a sheet pan and let cool for about 2 hours, until cool enough to handle. Pour the collected rib juices into an airtight container and refrigerate while the ribs cool.

5. Prepare the grill for high heat and lightly grease the grates with neutral oil (see page 65).

6. Use a spoon to scrape off and discard the layer of fat from the chilled rib juices. Scrape the gelatinized rib juices into a large saucepan and add the balsamic barbecue sauce. Set the saucepan on the grill and warm through until bubbling, about 6 minutes. Remove from the heat.

RECIPE CONTINUES

7. Unwrap the ribs and generously brush both sides with the barbecue sauce. Lay the racks on the grill. Close the lid and cook, flipping and brushing with more barbecue sauce every 5 minutes, about 15 minutes total. Remove from the heat and brush the top sides with another layer of sauce.

8. Let rest for 5 minutes before cutting between the ribs to separate. Arrange on a platter and serve with the remaining barbecue sauce on the side.

Note

To make this recipe in the oven, follow the same recipe for the first slow bake. Set the broiler to high. Place a rack in the top, 6 inches from the heat source. Brush the ribs generously with barbecue sauce and broil until the sauce begins to caramelize, about 4 minutes, checking halfway so they don't burn.

Dad's Grilled Swordfish *with* Pickled Salsa

Serves 8

I have spent a lot of time standing next to my dad while he's grilling everything under the sun, and this recipe has long been one of his favorites. Grilled fish is great, but it often ends up falling apart and getting stuck to the grates, which is a bigger headache than it's worth. Enter swordfish: its thick-cut steaks char beautifully without flaking apart. Thanks, Dad! As an extra insurance policy (dads *love* insurance policies), marinating them in a flavorful olive oil mixture makes sure the flesh is slick and ready to flip. Dad's a big fan of capers, so I like to make a briny, acidic salsa to complement it. A mix of onion, garlic, capers, and scallions quickly pickle in oil and vinegar while the fish does its thing—spooning it on top ensures every bite is bursting with flavor.

Make Ahead The swordfish can marinate up to 24 hours. The caper salsa can be refrigerated in an airtight container up to 3 days.

SWORDFISH

¼ cup extra-virgin olive oil

4 scallions, thinly sliced

8 garlic cloves, thinly sliced

2 teaspoons kosher salt

8 (1-inch-thick) swordfish fillets, 6 to 8 ounces each

PICKLED SALSA

1 small red onion, finely diced

¼ cup drained capers

4 scallions, thinly sliced

4 garlic cloves, thinly sliced

3 tablespoons white wine vinegar

2 tablespoons extra-virgin olive oil

½ teaspoon kosher salt

Neutral oil, for greasing

1. **MAKE THE SWORDFISH:** In a large zip-top bag or airtight container, combine the olive oil, scallions, garlic, and salt. Seal the bag and shake to mix the ingredients. Add the fillets to the bag and turn to coat. Seal and marinate in the fridge for at least 4 hours or up to 24 hours.

2. Prepare the grill for high heat and lightly grease the grates with neutral oil (see page 65).

3. **MAKE THE PICKLED SALSA:** In a small bowl, combine the red onion, capers, scallions, garlic, vinegar, olive oil, and salt to combine. Set aside to marinate while you grill.

4. Transfer the swordfish from the marinade directly onto the grill. (Let the excess drip off, but it's okay if pieces of scallion or garlic stick to the fish.) Close the lid and cook until the bottom is nicely charred, about 3 minutes. Flip, cover, and cook until the fish is just cooked through, about 3 minutes more. Transfer to a serving platter and let rest for about 5 minutes.

5. Serve the grilled swordfish with the bowl of caper salsa alongside for spooning onto each portion.

Note

To make this recipe on the stove, use a preheated large skillet, coated with 2 tablespoons neutral oil over medium heat. Working in batches, cook the fillets for about 4 minutes on each side.

DAD'S GRILLED SWORDFISH WITH PICKLED SALSA, PAGE 55

Grilled Pound Cake & Peaches

Serves 8

If you've ever ordered a grilled corn muffin from a diner—warm, buttery heaven!—then I'm sure you'll understand my obsession with grilling pound cake. It has the same rich, dense sweetness that gets even better as it heats up on the grill. For the ultimate mom hack, I use the Sara Lee pound cake hiding in my freezer. Here, ripe summer peaches get a bath of an unbeatable butter–brown sugar–cinnamon mixture so they caramelize beautifully, and that same sugar mixture doubles as a drizzly topping for bowls of those peaches with warm pound cake and big scoops of melting ice cream. This is what summer is all about: a simple, perfect dessert.

Neutral oil, for greasing

½ cup (I stick) unsalted butter

½ cup packed dark brown sugar

I teaspoon ground cinnamon

¼ teaspoon kosher salt

4 ripe peaches, halved and pitted

Fresh or thawed frozen pound cake, sliced into 8 pieces

Vanilla ice cream, for serving

Chopped raw pistachios, for serving (optional)

I. Prepare the grill for high heat and lightly grease the grates with neutral oil (see page 65).

2. In a small saucepan on the grill, melt the butter. Add the brown sugar, cinnamon, and salt. Whisk to form a smooth mixture, then remove from the grill.

3. Generously brush the cut sides of the peaches with the sugar mixture. Place the peaches cut side down on the grill, then brush the skin side with more of the sugar mixture. Close the lid and cook until charred on the cut sides, about 5 minutes. Transfer to a sheet pan, cut side up, and brush on a little more of the sugar mixture.

4. Return the saucepan to one side of the grill. Bring the sauce to simmer and cook to reduce slightly, about 4 minutes. Meanwhile, arrange the pound cake slices on the other side of the grill. Cook until marks appear on the surface, about 2 minutes per side, then transfer to the sheet pan. Pour the remaining sugar mixture into a small serving bowl and set on the sheet pan along with the ice cream and a bowl of chopped pistachios, if desired.

5. Bring the whole sheet pan to the table and let everyone assemble their own combos.

Note

To make this recipe in the oven, set the broiler to high. Place a rack in the top, 6 inches from the heat source. Line a rimmed sheet pan with foil and arrange the peach halves cut side up. Brush generously with the sugar mixture and broil until the sugar begins to caramelize, about 4 minutes, checking halfway so they don't burn.

GRILLED POUND CAKE & PEACHES, PAGE 58

Grossy P's Arnie P

Serves 8

I would estimate about 90 percent of my lifetime liquid intake has been Arnold Palmers. If I'm sitting in a restaurant, you can be sure his name is on the tip of my tongue. But the great news is, unlike most soft drinks, it's just as easy and delicious to make at home. (Take that, Diet Coke!) An Arnold Palmer is a simple blend of lemonade and iced tea, so I make a big batch of each, stir them together in a pitcher, and keep it cold in my fridge. My personal dream ratio is 75 percent tea and 25 percent lemonade, so this recipe reflects that exact mix for a perfectly tart and tannic drink, but feel free to adjust your ratio to your taste buds' delight.

Make Ahead The lemonade and iced tea can be refrigerated in an airtight container up to 1 week.

LEMONADE

½ cup sugar

¾ cup fresh lemon juice (from 3 to 4 lemons)

ICED TEA

6 black tea bags

FOR SERVING

Ice

Mint sprigs

Lemon wheels

1. **MAKE THE LEMONADE:** In a medium saucepan, combine 1 cup water with the sugar. Bring to a boil over high heat and cook, stirring occasionally, until the sugar is dissolved, 1 to 2 minutes. Remove from the heat and immediately add 2 cups cold water. Set aside to cool for 30 minutes.

2. In a pitcher or Mason jar, stir the sugar water with the lemon juice to combine.

3. **MEANWHILE, MAKE THE ICED TEA:** In the same saucepan (no need to wipe it out), bring 2 cups water to a boil over high heat. Remove from the heat and add the tea bags. Steep for 5 minutes, then discard the tea bags and immediately add 2 cups cold water. Set aside to cool for 30 minutes. Pour into the pitcher with the lemonade. The drink can be served immediately or chilled until ready to use.

4. To serve, fill glasses with plenty of ice, then pour in the Arnold Palmers. Garnish each with a big sprig of mint, a lemon wheel, and a colorful straw.

Note

I like my Arnold Palmers tart, so my lemonade is light on sugar. If you're a sweet tea drinker, use ¾ cup of sugar when making the lemonade.

Grossy's Guide *Grilling*

When I yell "Let's grill, girls!" I don't mean let's take a pic by the flames, post it on Instagram, and then let someone else man the burgers (read: Gus). Okay, maybe sometimes that's what I mean, but most of the time I mean let's actually grill, girls!!! Being a grill girl is way easier than it seems, and here's everything you need to know.

Tool Kit

There are a few must-haves before you get started. Grillers at every level should invest in:

GRILL BRUSH: A sturdy wire brush is the old standby. The bristles will burn over time, so get a cheap one and expect to replace it every year or two. If you're wary of brush bristles getting stuck on the grill, Scrub Daddy makes a grill sponge that does a great job getting the grates clean.

HEAVY GLOVES: The grill gets very hot, so keeping your hands protected makes flipping, basting, and seasoning more enjoyable. It also makes handling any skillets or saucepans on the grill a total breeze.

LONG TONGS: Keep your arm hair safe! Look for long tongs with a wooden or silicone handle, which stays cool to the touch. Metal handles look sleek but will spread the heat to your hands.

GRILL CHIMNEY: This one's a must for charcoal grills. Just stuff some crumpled newspaper in the bottom, load the top with charcoal, and light up. In about 15 minutes, you'll have perfectly white-hot coals ready to pour in the bottom of the grill and work their magic.

INSTANT-READ THERMOMETER: Indoors or out, the only way to be sure your meat is cooked through without drying out is to take its temperature.

RIMMED SHEET PANS: A small stack of sheet pans will help you transport everything you need outside, give you a place to rest grilled meat, and can even travel to the table for serving.

HAND WIPES: Even if it's just a wet kitchen towel, give yourself something to wipe sauce off your hands so you don't have to run back inside while the flames are roaring.

BAKING SODA: You're going to want an economy-size box, and here's why: If your grill starts flaring up, the first step is removing the food, then close the grill lid and see if the fire subsides. If it's still aggressive, turn off the burners and close the lid again. If it's really stubborn, blanket the flames in baking soda to extinguish. You'll probably never need to use it, but it's good to have on hand.

Lighting Up

To light a charcoal grill, fill the chimney with charcoal and stuff the base with torn up newspaper, love letters, paper towels, napkins, or anything flammable. Set the chimney on the grill grates and light the paper. The paper will ignite the bottom coals, and the heat will slowly rise until the top of the coals are white-hot.

To light a gas grill, first be sure your propane tank is full. (Ideally, check this the day before.) Next, open the grill lid so any excess gas can escape—no fireballs here! Twist the tank open so the gas starts flowing. Working one burner at a time, turn the knob to high or the flame symbol. Push the ignition button next to the knobs until you see the flame ignite. Repeat, working down the row. Now we're cooking with gas, as they say!

Temperature Control

Just like your oven, a grill needs time to preheat, usually 10 to 15 minutes. Depending on the recipe, you might need high or medium heat, with direct or indirect zones. Here's what that all means:

● CHARCOAL

HIGH HEAT: When the coals are hot, spread them across the entire base of the grill. Open the top and bottom vents completely. Cover the grill and heat for at least 10 minutes, aiming for about 500°F.

MEDIUM HEAT: When the coals are hot, spread them across the entire base of the grill. Open the top vent completely and the bottom vent halfway. Cover the grill and heat for at least 10 minutes, aiming for about 350°F.

INDIRECT AND DIRECT HEAT: Once the coals are hot, pile them along half of the base of the grill. Follow the same instructions for high or medium heat. When it's time to grill, the coals are your direct heat zone; the half without is the indirect heat zone.

● GAS

HIGH HEAT: Turn all the burners to high. Cover the grill and heat for at least 10 minutes, aiming for about 500°F.

MEDIUM HEAT: Turn all the burners to medium. Cover the grill and heat for at least 10 minutes, aiming for about 350°F.

INDIRECT AND DIRECT HEAT: Ignite the burners on one side of the grill only, leaving the other burners off. Follow the same instructions for high or medium heat. When it's time to grill, the lit burners are your direct heat zone; the unlit side is the indirect heat zone.

Liftoff

Preheated grates will give you a pretty good nonstick surface, but for a truly easy breezy experience, they need two more things before you lay your food down.

Once the grill is at the correct temperature, use a grill brush to give the grates a good swipe, just in case any bits are stuck on from the last time it was used. They don't need to be sparkling clean, just free from any visible char.

After exfoliating, we moisturize. A light coat of neutral oil will ensure your food releases with zero effort. But big drips will cause flare-ups, so easy does it. Wad up a couple of paper towels and use tongs to lightly dip them (don't dunk!) in some neutral oil. Use the tongs to wipe the towel along the grates until they're glistening. Remember, your food will tell you when it's ready for a flip; grill until it builds enough of a char to self-release.

As soon as one batch of food comes off the grill, give the grates another scrub with the brush and swipe with the towel before the next. After cooking, turn off the grill and give the hot grates one more good rub to get rid of any stuck-on bits.

Dips in the Pool

Make THE *Menu*

● **2 DAYS BEFORE**

Labneh Tzatziki: Mix and strain yogurt to make the labneh.

● **1 DAY BEFORE**

Beany Bikini Dip: Make the dip and store in the fridge.

Stone Fruit Salsa: Make the salsa and store in the fridge.

Mollie's Peanut Butter Dip: Make the dip and store in the fridge.

GET READY TO DIVE INTO ONE OF MY FAVORITE

food groups: dips. I feel most alive when I step into the role of vacation house mom. When my friends and I rent a place, preferably with a pool, preferably on Fire Island, I can't help but go into full domestic goddess mode.

Needless to say, I'm always the person in charge of the food for any extended stay, and I ensure we have a proper breakfast and dinner every day. But lunch is where the magic of dips comes in. A lazy afternoon with a spread of snacky dips by the pool is the perfect way to feed a group on a hot day.

While my boys are splashing in the pool, I'm in the kitchen whipping up bowl after bowl of goodness. The collection on this menu is fresh and easy, and the best part is they can all be made ahead and kept in the fridge all week to add to all your other meals. Grab your party-size bag of chips and let's make a spread that'll have everyone diving in for more!

Labneh Tzatziki: Make the dip and store in the fridge.

Black-and-White Mascarpone Dip: Make the dip and store in the fridge.

Watermelon Lime Slushie: Cut up the watermelon and freeze.

● **SERVING TIME**

Watermelon Lime Slushie: Prepare glasses and blend the drinks.

Arrange dips on platters with appropriate garnishes and dippers.

Beany Bikini Dip

Makes 2 cups

In colder months, I become obsessed with beans in any way, shape, or form. What are they doing at the pool wearing a bikini, you ask? One of my favorite bean tricks is turning them into a thick, creamy, and refreshing dip. (Plus, everyone knows that a pool is the best place to secretly fart.) Blending cannellini beans with yogurt makes everything smooth and delicious, and adding a roasted beet gives it a stunning, summer-worthy neon-pink color and sweet, earthy flavor. A final touch of chopped pistachios and a drizzle of olive oil makes taking a dip irresistible.

Make Ahead The dip can be refrigerated in an airtight container up to 3 days; garnish just before serving.

I small red beet, trimmed and scrubbed

½ cup plain full-fat Greek yogurt

I (15.5-ounce) can cannellini beans, drained and rinsed

2 tablespoons fresh lemon juice

I tablespoon white wine vinegar

I garlic clove, grated

Kosher salt and freshly ground black pepper

Chopped pistachios, for serving

Extra-virgin olive oil, for serving

I. Preheat the oven to 450°F.

2. Tightly wrap the beet in foil. Set on a rimmed sheet pan and bake for 45 to 50 minutes until a knife easily slides in and out. Unwrap the beet and let cool until easy to handle. Rub with paper towels to peel the skin off and then roughly chop.

3. In a food processor, combine the roasted beet, yogurt, cannellini beans, lemon juice, vinegar, garlic, and a good pinch each of salt and pepper. Process, stopping to scrape down the sides as needed, until combined and smooth, I to 2 minutes. Taste for seasoning and add more salt and pepper as needed.

4. Transfer to a medium bowl, smoothing into a mostly even layer with some peaks and valleys. Garnish with chopped pistachios, more black pepper, and a drizzle of olive oil before serving.

WHAT TO DIP IN IT: *Crudités, toasted baguette slices, or pitas.*

OTHER USES: *Sandwich spread, roasted or grilled meats and vegetables.*

Stone Fruit Salsa

Makes 3 cups

At some point during my childhood, my mom and I discovered Stonewall Kitchen's peach salsa, and it was love at first bite. It became a Pelosi family staple, especially on family vacations, and we bought enough jars that you'd think we owned stock in the company. So to no one's surprise (or at least, not my mom's), my favorite use for overly ripe stone fruit is this simple, chunky dip that mimics the Stonewall version. As a certified sweet-and-savory girlie, this salsa hits every time.

Make Ahead The salsa can be refrigerated in an airtight container up to 3 days.

½ pound stone fruit, such as peaches, plums, apricots, or a mix, pitted and diced

I pound vine tomatoes, diced

I tablespoon apple cider vinegar

Kosher salt

I medium white onion, quartered

I jalapeño, halved and seeded

2 garlic cloves, smashed

2 tablespoons neutral oil

½ cup fresh cilantro leaves

Juice of I lime

I. Preheat the broiler to high.

2. In a large bowl, combine the stone fruit and tomatoes with the apple cider vinegar and a big pinch of salt. Toss to combine, then set aside to macerate.

3. On a rimmed sheet pan, toss the onion, jalapeño, and garlic with the neutral oil and a big pinch of salt. Broil, checking often, until charred all over, 5 to 10 minutes.

4. Transfer the charred vegetables to a food processor and add the cilantro and lime juice. Pulse 2 to 4 times just to break down the ingredients. Add the peaches and tomatoes, along with any collected liquid, and pulse 2 more times to make a chunky salsa with uneven pieces.

5. Transfer the salsa to the same large bowl, taste for seasoning, and add more salt as needed before serving.

WHAT TO DIP IN IT: *Tortilla chips.*

OTHER USES: *Grilled fish, grilled meat, tacos, and avocado toast.*

Mollie's Peanut Butter Dip

Makes 2¼ cups

Shortly after moving to NYC, I became friends with Sam Black, who one day casually mentioned that his mom is Mollie Katzen. If you don't know (and I bet you do), she's the legend behind the *Moosewood Cookbook*. After some ~~outright begging~~ friendly persuasion, I got to meet Mollie, who is now a great friend and mentor. At a dinner celebrating the legacy of Moosewood, I tasted this peanut sauce–inspired dip, and it whisked me right back to my favorite childhood snack of peanut butter and celery. After some more ~~outright begging~~ friendly persuasion, Mollie graciously let me adapt her recipe for you, so here's my take on a perfect blend of nostalgia and exciting new flavors.

Make Ahead The dip can be refrigerated in an airtight container up to 3 days.

I cup smooth peanut butter	¼ cup minced fresh cilantro leaves
I cup boiling water	6 garlic cloves, minced
¼ cup soy sauce	2 teaspoons apple cider vinegar
¼ cup packed dark brown sugar	I teaspoon sriracha
	Kosher salt

I. In a medium bowl, stir together the peanut butter and boiling water until completely smooth and incorporated. Add the soy sauce, sugar, cilantro, garlic, apple cider vinegar, and sriracha. Taste for seasoning and add salt as needed.

2. Cover the bowl tightly with cling wrap and refrigerate for at least 2 hours or overnight. Bring to room temperature before serving.

WHAT TO DIP IN IT: *Crudités, pretzels, or apple slices.*

OTHER USES: *Grilled chicken, grilled fish, noodles, salad dressing (diluted).*

Labneh Tzatziki

Makes 2 cups

Mediterranean restaurants are my dip heaven. Nothing is better than soft triangles of pita surrounded by a smattering of small bowls. I especially love tart labneh covered in olive oil and creamy tzatziki packed with herbs. This recipe borrows the best of both dips—labneh's thickness and tang with tzatziki's cooling cucumber, dill, and mint—and combines them to make my version of a delightfully refreshing dip.

Make Ahead The ungarnished tzatziki can be refrigerated in an airtight container up to 3 days.

LABNEH	Juice of I lemon
2 cups plain full-fat Greek yogurt	Freshly ground black pepper
¼ teaspoon kosher salt	¼ cup chopped fresh dill, plus more for serving
TZATZIKI	¼ cup chopped fresh mint, plus more for serving
I large English cucumber	
½ teaspoon kosher salt, plus more to taste	Extra-virgin olive oil, for serving
I garlic clove, grated	

I. **MAKE THE LABNEH:** In a medium bowl, mix the Greek yogurt and salt. Line a colander with two layers of cheesecloth, leaving some overhang all around. Scrape the yogurt mixture into the center and cover with the overhang. Set the colander in a large bowl and refrigerate for at least 24 hours or up to 48 hours for extra-thick labneh. Finished labneh can be refrigerated in an airtight container for up to 2 weeks.

2. **MAKE THE TZATZIKI:** Grate the cucumber on the large holes of a box grater or using a food processor. Transfer to a colander and toss with ½ teaspoon of salt. Let drain for 15 minutes to release some moisture.

3. Meanwhile, in a large bowl, combine the garlic and lemon juice. When the cucumber is done draining, add it to the bowl along with the labneh and a big pinch each of salt and pepper. Mix well to combine, then stir in the dill and mint. Taste for seasoning and add more salt as needed. Garnish with a drizzle of olive oil and a sprinkle of dill and mint before serving.

WHAT TO DIP IN IT: *Pitas, pita chips, or crudités.*

OTHER USES: *Perfect with grilled meat, fish, or vegetables. Or as a spread on sandwiches or tomato toast.*

Black-and-White Mascarpone Dip

Makes 2½ cups

Enjoying freshly cut up fruit in hot weather is one of my greatest pleasures. Dipping that fruit in this irresistibly fluffy dip is pure bliss. Think of it as an upgraded version of the Fluff and cream cheese combo we all grew up eating (and that my sister, Diana, a true queen, still makes). Rich mascarpone is whipped with heavy cream and powdered sugar until it's sweet and airy. That would be enough for a big bowl of fun, but I like to mix half of it with Nutella for the kind of double-dipping that's actually encouraged.

Make Ahead The dip can be refrigerated in an airtight container up to 3 days; bring to room temperature before serving.

½ cup powdered sugar

½ cup heavy cream

1 teaspoon pure vanilla extract

2 (8-ounce) containers mascarpone cheese, at room temperature

¼ cup Nutella

1. In a medium bowl, combine ¼ cup of the powdered sugar, ¼ cup of the heavy cream, and the vanilla. Use a handheld mixer on low speed or a whisk to beat until the sugar is fully incorporated, about 2 minutes. Add half the mascarpone and beat again until incorporated and the mixture is airy, 1 to 2 minutes. Scoop the mixture into one side of a shallow serving bowl and smooth the top into an even layer.

2. In the same medium bowl (no need to wipe it out), combine the remaining ¼ cup powdered sugar and the heavy cream. Use a handheld mixer on low speed or a whisk to beat until the sugar is fully incorporated, about 2 minutes. Add the remaining mascarpone along with the Nutella and beat again until incorporated and the mixture is airy, 1 to 2 minutes. Scoop the mixture into the other side of the serving bowl and smooth the top into an even layer, creating a line down the center, before serving.

WHAT TO DIP IN IT: *Nilla wafers, pretzels, cut-up fruit.*

OTHER USES: *Spread it on toast, pancakes, or French toast. Top ice cream with it.*

Watermelon Lime Slushie

Makes 4 drinks

My sister and I spent most of our childhood summers begging our parents for two things: a pool in our backyard and a slushie from the 7-Eleven down the street. Since we had no actual space to put a pool, we settled for an endless supply of slushies. Now, whenever I find myself within the radius of a pool, this is all I want to sip. Watermelon freezes so beautifully that it basically becomes flavored ice all on its own. Add in a little sugar and lime to blend it up, a little honey and salt on the rim, maybe a vodka or tequila floater on top, and this is a grown-up drink for the young at heart.

Make Ahead The watermelon can be frozen up to 24 hours; blend just before serving.

1 (3-pound) wedge of watermelon, rind removed and cut into ½-inch cubes, or 2 pounds cubed watermelon

½ cup sugar

¼ cup fresh lime juice (from 2 to 3 limes)

FOR SERVING

Honey or agave

Flaky sea salt

Fresh mint sprigs

1. Place the watermelon in a large zip-top bag or airtight container and freeze for at least 4 hours or overnight.

2. Place rocks glasses in the freezer to chill. In a blender, combine the frozen watermelon, sugar, lime juice, and ½ cup water. Let the watermelon thaw for 15 minutes for easy blending. Blend on high speed until smooth, stopping to stir as needed, about 2 minutes.

3. Pour some honey onto a small plate and spread some flaky salt on a separate small plate. Dip the rim of each rocks glass into the honey, then swirl in the salt. Divide the watermelon slush among the glasses, garnish with mint sprigs, and serve cold.

Tomato Girl Summer

Make THE *Menu*

● **2 DAYS BEFORE**

Tomato Pie: Make the pie and store in the fridge.

Sweet Tomato Granita: Make the granita and freeze.

My Best Friend Mary: Make the bloody mix and store in the fridge.

● **1 DAY BEFORE**

Tuscan Panzanella Salad: Toast the bread and store at room temperature.

Sunshine Pasta: Make the pasta and store in the fridge until ready to serve, if serving chilled.

YOU KNOW THAT BOARD GAME, OPERATION?

If it were based on me, you'd see a tomato where my heart should be. Some of my earliest memories are of my family's late-summer harvest, when tomatoes are so ripe they could burst. It felt as magical as Christmas morning. All tomatoes are good tomatoes—fresh, frozen, or canned—but the aroma and oozing juices of a freshly picked one are incomparable.

Growing up in an Italian American family means tomatoes are at every meal. Raw, sliced, and salted is perfection, but we also put tomatoes through their paces as sauces, salads, soups, and sides. It's impossible to run out of ideas because they shine anywhere you put them. The recipes in this chapter will help expand your repertoire with apps, mains, and even a sweet dessert. (Don't forget, the tomato is technically a fruit!)

Using the freshest tomatoes you can get your hands on will obviously guarantee the best results. But if you're just dying to crack open a can, or the grocery store beefsteak is really calling your name, I completely understand. After all, my body is 60 percent marinara pumping through my tomato heart.

● **1 HOUR BEFORE**

Tomato Pie: Remove from the fridge to come to room temperature.

Sunshine Pasta: Remove from the fridge, if serving at room temperature.

● **15 MINUTES BEFORE**

Tuscan Panzanella Salad: Toss the tomatoes and onions to marinate.

Flank Steak with Tomato Chimichurri: Make the chimichurri and grill the steak.

● **SERVING TIME**

Tuscan Panzanella Salad: Add the bread to the salad.

Flank Steak with Tomato Chimichurri: Slice the steak and assemble the platter.

My Best Friend Mary: Set out the bloody mix and garnishes.

Sweet Tomato Granita: Serve the granita for dessert.

Tuscan Panzanella Salad

Serves 6 to 8

I've always said panzanella salad is just a bread basket in drag. It's the same satisfying taste of ripping apart a dinner roll and running it through vinegary oil but dressed up for the evening gown portion of the night. This salad began as Tuscan peasant food, a very smart way to get an extra meal out of stale loaves. Now you'll find it with luxury accessories like cheese, stone fruits, or all kinds of proteins. She is the original Mother of the House of Panzanzella, and her authenticity speaks for itself. When the tomatoes mingle with onions, red wine vinegar, oil, and plenty of salt and pepper, you've got everything you need in the world. Waiting until the very last minute to toss in the toasted bread means you'll get that balance of crunchy and soft, saturated bites that make this salad so perfect.

Make Ahead The bread can be toasted and stored in an airtight container at room temperature up to 3 days.

3 pounds heirloom tomatoes, cut into 1-inch pieces

Kosher salt and freshly ground black pepper

1 large red onion, cut into 1-inch pieces

¼ cup red wine vinegar

¼ cup extra-virgin olive oil, plus more for drizzling

1 (16-ounce) loaf crusty bread, torn into 1-inch pieces

1. Preheat the oven to 400°F.

2. Place the tomatoes (and any collected juices from the cutting board) in a large bowl and add a few big pinches of salt and plenty of pepper. Toss gently to mix. Add the onion along with the vinegar and olive oil. Toss again.

3. On a rimmed sheet pan, drizzle the bread with a little bit of olive oil and toss to coat. Toast in the oven for about 10 minutes, until lightly golden. Remove and let the bread cool on the sheet pan, about 15 minutes.

4. Just before serving, add the bread to the bowl and toss to coat in the juices. Taste for seasoning and serve immediately.

Tomato Pie

Serves 6 to 8

Tomato + mayonnaise = one of the all-time great love stories (see page 91 for more on that). But tomatoes + mayonnaise with a bit of mustard, mixed with cheese, and baked in a flaky pie crust? That's the kind of relationship that makes me consider leaving Gus. Just kidding. Kind of. Sort of a cross between a pizza and a quiche, tomato pie is a perfectly summery appetizer or a light main course. Even though it's a Southern specialty, it fits right in on my Italian American table.

Make Ahead The pie can be baked, cooled, wrapped tightly, and refrigerated up to 3 days.

CRUST

1½ cups all-purpose flour, plus more for rolling

2 teaspoons sugar

½ teaspoon kosher salt

½ cup (I stick) unsalted butter, cubed

2 to 3 tablespoons ice water

FILLING

2 medium heirloom tomatoes, thickly sliced

Kosher salt and freshly ground black pepper

½ cup mayonnaise

I large egg

I tablespoon spicy brown mustard

I cup shredded mozzarella cheese

I cup shredded extra-sharp cheddar cheese

½ cup freshly grated Parmesan cheese

2 scallions, thinly sliced, plus more for serving

I. **MAKE THE CRUST:** In a food processor, combine the flour, sugar, and salt. Pulse two times just to mix. Add the butter and process until a rough dough forms, about 30 seconds. Add 2 tablespoons of the ice water and process until the dough pulls together. If needed, add another tablespoon water. Press the dough into a disc and wrap tightly with cling wrap. Refrigerate for at least 2 hours or up to 2 days.

2. Lightly dust a work surface with flour. Roll out the pie dough, adding more flour as needed, into a 12-inch circle. Transfer the dough to a 9-inch pie plate and crimp the edges. Chill the crust in the freezer for 30 minutes.

3. Meanwhile, preheat the oven to 400°F.

4. Remove the crust from the freezer. Cover with parchment paper and fill with pie weights or dried beans. Bake for about 30 minutes, until the bottom and edges are golden brown. Remove the weights and parchment and let the crust cool completely, about I hour.

5. **MEANWHILE MAKE THE FILLING:** Arrange the tomato slices on a paper towel–lined plate and season generously with salt and pepper. Let the tomatoes get nice and juicy at room temperature until the crust is cool.

6. In a medium bowl, whisk the mayonnaise, egg, and mustard. Stir in the mozzarella, cheddar, Parmesan, and scallion. Spread half the cheese mixture on the bottom of the crust, then add some of the tomato slices in an even layer. Repeat with the remaining ingredients, then finish with another sprinkle of scallions.

7. Bake for 35 to 40 minutes, until the filling is puffy but feels set when lightly pressed. Remove from the oven and cool for at least I hour before slicing and serving.

Sunshine Pasta

Serves 6 to 8

No one appreciates a bubbling pot of marinara more than I do. But when summer comes and the sun is on high heat, the last place you're going to find me is standing over the stove for hours at a time. This is my go-to no-cook sauce when I'm in vacation mode and "AC" and "iced tea" are the only words I want to hear. In fact, the only things sweating here are the beautifully orange, extra-sweet Sungold tomatoes. Get them started with salt so their juices easily coat the hot pasta, then mix in fresh oregano, grated Parmesan, and plenty of olive oil for the easiest dinner you'll ever make. It's delicious hot or at room temperature, but it's possibly even better for lunch the next day as a cold pasta salad.

Make Ahead *The finished pasta can be cooled, covered, and refrigerated up to 24 hours.*

2 pounds Sungold tomatoes, quartered

Kosher salt

1 pound dried orecchiette pasta

½ cup lightly packed fresh oregano leaves

½ cup freshly grated Parmesan cheese

½ cup extra-virgin olive oil

1. In a large bowl, toss the tomatoes with a few good pinches of salt. Set aside the tomatoes at room temperature to release their delicious juices.

2. Meanwhile, bring a large pot of salted water to a boil over high heat. Add the pasta and cook until al dente according to the package directions. Reserve 1 cup of the pasta cooking water, then drain.

3. Add the pasta and about ¼ cup of the reserved pasta cooking water to the bowl with the tomatoes and fold to mix well. Add the oregano, Parmesan, and olive oil. Fold again, adding another splash of pasta water as needed to make a smooth sauce that coats the pasta. Serve hot, let cool to room temperature, or refrigerate overnight before serving.

Flank Steak *with* Tomato Chimichurri

Serves 6 to 8

Gus is my boyfriend, but he is also my grill friend (sorry), and a perfectly charred steak is one of our favorite summer dinners. When cherry tomatoes are bright red and ripe, I love making this herby tomato chimichurri while Gus tends to the flames. A mix of lemon and vinegar, roughly chopped herbs, a few glugs of olive oil, and a pile of sweet-tart tomatoes are perfect for cutting through the rich meat. And because we're usually making this dinner on the fly, I skip the marinade and spoon the chimichurri over the sliced steak to let all the juices soak and mingle together as we eat.

Zest and juice of I lemon

2 tablespoons red wine vinegar

Extra-virgin olive oil

Kosher salt and freshly ground black pepper

I pound cherry tomatoes, halved

¼ cup chopped fresh parsley

2 tablespoons chopped fresh basil

Neutral oil, for greasing

2 pounds flank steak

1. In a large bowl, whisk together the lemon zest, lemon juice, vinegar, 2 tablespoons olive oil, and I teaspoon each salt and pepper. Add the tomatoes, parsley, and basil and toss to combine.

2. Prepare the grill for high heat and lightly grease the grates with neutral oil (see page 65).

3. Rub both sides of the flank steak with a generous drizzle of olive oil, then season with salt and pepper. Lay the steak on the grates. Close the lid and cook until charred, about 8 minutes, flipping halfway through.

4. Transfer the steak to a cutting board and let rest for about 5 minutes. Slice against the grain in ½-inch-thick pieces and arrange on a serving platter. Spoon the tomato mixture over the steak and around the platter. Finish with a few more grinds of pepper before serving.

Note
To make this recipe on the stove, use a preheated large cast-iron skillet over medium-high heat, coated with I tablespoon of neutral oil. Cook the steak for 2 to 3 minutes on each side.

SWEET TOMATO GRANITA, PAGE 86

Sweet Tomato Granita

Makes 1 pint

I know what you are thinking: Only an Italian American would make a dessert out of tomato. But there is a sweetness to peak-summer tomatoes that makes sense here. (It's helped along by a little bit more sugar, of course.) Granita is so easy to make: All you do is blend three ingredients together and occasionally scrape the mixture as it freezes. For such a simple recipe, the reward is huge, with a delicate and refreshing finish to any steamy summer day.

Make Ahead   *The granita can be frozen up to 1 week.*

I pound ripe cherry tomatoes

¼ cup sugar

½ teaspoon kosher salt

I. In a blender, combine the tomatoes, sugar, and salt. Blend on high speed until a pulpy mixture forms, about 2 minutes. Pour into a large airtight container or 9 × 5-inch loaf pan.

2. Freeze for 2 hours, until partly frozen, then use a fork to mash into a thick, frosty mix. Freeze for 2 more hours, then use the fork to scrape and mash into crystals. Freeze for at least 4 more hours or overnight. Just before serving, scrape and mash again to make a soft icy mixture.

3. Scoop into small bowls and serve cold.

My Best Friend Mary

Makes 4 cups

Before my sister Diana's wedding, her groom, Bill, invited me to Las Vegas for his bachelor party. Shortly after we landed in Vegas, we hit the bar and after everyone had ordered their beers and shots, I ordered a Bloody Mary . . . at 11:00 p.m. on a Friday. I explained to the extremely confused (and straight) group of Bill's friends that I'm not a big drinker, but I love a Bloody Mary because it reminds me of marinara sauce. They all laughed, and it turned out to be the perfect ice breaker for a *very* fun weekend. What happens in Vegas stays in Vegas, but my love of a cold Mary follows me everywhere. Starting my mix with fresh tomatoes makes for a perfectly thick, saucy glass of fun.

Make Ahead The bloody mix can be refrigerated up to 48 hours.

2 pounds ripe cherry tomatoes

¼ cup fresh lemon juice (from I to 2 lemons)

I garlic clove

3 tablespoons prepared horseradish

I tablespoon kosher salt

I tablespoon soy sauce or Worcestershire sauce

I teaspoon freshly ground black pepper

½ teaspoon hot sauce, such as Tabasco or sriracha (optional)

I cup ice, plus more for serving

Celery stalks, for serving

Pitted or stuffed olives, for serving

I. In a blender, combine the tomatoes, lemon juice, garlic and ¼ cup water. Blend on high speed until smooth, about 2 minutes. Pour the mixture into a pitcher. Stir in the horseradish, salt, soy sauce, pepper, and hot sauce (if using). Stir the ice into the pitcher and refrigerate until the ice is melted and the mixture is chilled, at least 2 hours but preferably overnight.

2. To serve, fill tall glasses with ice. Pour about ½ cup of the Bloody Mary mix into each glass. Garnish with a celery stalk. Spear some olives on toothpicks and rest them on the edge of each glass before serving.

MY BEST FRIEND MARY, PAGE 87

Grossy's Guide Tomatoes

If you know anything about me, you know I really love tomatoes. That is because I have told you over and over again that I love tomatoes! Give me a thick, juicy tomato, and you'll see true happiness in action. Ask me about tomatoes, and I simply will not shut up. Allow me to prove it to you in this guide to all things tomatoes.

You Say Tomato, I Say What Kind?

Beefsteak These are the big boys. They're meaty, juicy, and ready to star in your sandwiches, burgers, or the world's best BLT. Beefsteaks are at their absolute peak June through September, when they can live their best lives under the sun. Look for tomatoes that are heavy for their size, firm but with a little give, and with skin that's smooth and vibrant.

Heirloom Heirloom tomatoes are like the quirky, asymmetrical haircut girls—they come in all shapes, colors, and sizes, and these beauties may have some funky shapes or cracks, but that's just their way of saying "I've got personality!" They're best eaten in their natural state, so let them shine raw in your salads, caprese, or just sliced and drizzled with olive oil and flaky salt. Heirlooms hit their stride in late summer, July through September. Look for firm tomatoes with a little give, bright coloring, and a sweet, earthy aroma.

Tiny Tomatoes Cherry, grape, Sungold, and other adorably small tomatoes are basically the M&M's of the tomato world. You pop one in your mouth, then another, and suddenly, you've happily eaten half the pint with no regrets. Sweet, bite-size, and juicy, they're perfect for throwing in salads, roasting with some olive oil, or just snacking on straight from the container. These babies are peak summer cuteness, so get them when they're plump and shiny—wrinkles are a red flag.

Vine Tomatoes Vine-ripened tomatoes love a little drama—they're literally still clinging to their codependent relationship with the vine. To guarantee next-level juiciness, look for late-summer tomatoes that are firm with a bright green, fresh-looking vine. (Wrinkly tomatoes and a dried-out vine are a pass.) Dice them, roast them, or make sauce out of them . . . you really can't mess these up.

Canned Tomatoes Canned tomatoes are your dependable BFF who always shows up, no matter what. They're processed and packed at their peak, so you know their flavor will be on point. San Marzano tomatoes are the royalty here, with the ideal balance of sweetness and acidity, but, honestly, any high-quality canned tomato will be perfect for all your saucy situations. Take a note from Bimpy and keep a stash in your pantry at all times.

Tomato TLC

Here's the golden rule: Never refrigerate your tomatoes! The cold air stops the ripening process and makes them mealy and bland. Store tomatoes on the counter, stem side down and out of direct sunlight to let them ripen naturally. Keep them away from other fruits and vegetables that give off ethylene (like bananas and avocados), a gas that will make them spoil.

Cutting Edge

Always use a serrated knife when cutting tomatoes. Regular knives are rarely sharp enough to glide through delicate tomato skin, so they'll squish these beauties into a sad, mushy mess. Serrated knives have saw-like teeth that slice with ease, preserving that plump shape and perfect, juicy interior.

Salt, Salt, Salt

The most important thing you can do to your tomato is properly salt it. The salt pulls out the juices in the tomato and brings them to the surface, which instantly enhances its flavor. I like to use flaky sea salt for this, which adds a nice crunch.

● TOMATO TOAST

For my whole life, summers have always meant picking tomatoes from Bimpy's garden and layering thick slices on bread. My go-to tomato toast combines bread, mayo, and tomato, but I've experimented with various tasty twists. For the bread, any type works, but I prefer thick slices of sourdough, multigrain, or even bagels, toasted to crispy perfection. For spreads, truly anything spreadable will be delicious. My faves include cream cheese, cottage cheese, pesto, and hummus. Slice ripe tomatoes—whatever kind you have—and sprinkle with flaky salt. Add extras like freshly ground black pepper or chili crisp. Top with proteins like bacon, anchovies, or a soft-boiled egg. And now, please join me in a toast to summer!

Breakfast for Dinner

Make THE *Menu*

● **1 DAY BEFORE**

Maple Bacon Brussels Sprouts: Cut the bacon and sprouts. Store separately in the fridge.

Scallion Cheddar Hash Brown Patties: Cook the patties and store in the fridge.

Diner Omelets for a Crowd: Assemble the omelets and store in the fridge.

● **THE NIGHT BEFORE**

Raisin Walnut Baked French Toast: Assemble the French toast and store in the fridge.

● **1 HOUR BEFORE**

Raisin Walnut Baked French Toast: Bake the French toast and cover with foil to keep warm.

Blackberry Lemon Dutch Baby: Make the batter.

WHEN I WAS A KID, NOTHING WAS MORE THRILLING than hearing the magic words, "Let's have breakfast for dinner!" Even though everyone around me keeps telling me I'm an adult and adults can make their own choices, having breakfast after dark still feels like I'm getting away with something scandalous, and it's one of my favorite things.

Every mom knows breakfast for dinner is just the easy way out, but my menu puts an intentional spin on the dinner party with recipes that are fun, unexpected, and surprisingly easy to make for a crowd. Of course, these recipes don't just have to be for dinner! They can be served for breakfast, lunch, or brunch. But the casual, relaxed vibe of a breakfast-for-dinner party is my favorite way to break away from the norm, making the party extra memorable and enjoyable for everyone. Can you imagine a better dinner invitation?

● 30 MINUTES BEFORE	● 15 MINUTES BEFORE	● 5 MINUTES BEFORE	● SERVING TIME
Diner Omelets for a Crowd: Bake the omelets and cover with foil to keep warm.	**Maple Bacon Brussels Sprouts:** Make the bacon and sprouts.	**Scallion Cheddar Hash Brown Patties:** Rewarm the patties.	**Blackberry Lemon Dutch Baby:** Spoon the topping over the Dutch baby.
	Blackberry Lemon Dutch Baby: Bake the Dutch baby, make the topping, and warm the maple syrup.		**Sunrise Mom-osas:** Assemble the drinks and serve.

Maple Bacon Brussels Sprouts

Serves 8

I'm a douse-my-bacon-in-syrup kind of breakfast girlie, so why stop there? Brussels sprouts crash this party in the most delicious way, having a morning-after ménage à trois with America's sweethearts: bacon and maple syrup. This brunchy love triangle is the perfect way to add some evening greens to the breakfast table magic. Grab that syrup and let's get sticky!

1 pound thick-cut bacon, cut into 1-inch pieces

2 tablespoons light brown sugar

1½ pounds Brussels sprouts, trimmed and halved

Kosher salt and freshly ground black pepper

3 tablespoons white balsamic vinegar or fresh lemon juice

3 tablespoons pure maple syrup

1. Arrange the bacon evenly in a large skillet and set over medium heat. Cook, flipping occasionally, until the fat has rendered and the bacon is just beginning to brown but is not quite crisp, about 8 minutes. Transfer the bacon to paper towels to drain, reserving the fat in the skillet.

2. Stir the brown sugar into the bacon fat, then immediately add the Brussels sprouts along with a good pinch each of salt and pepper. Toss to coat, then arrange so the cut sides are facing down. Cook over medium heat, undisturbed, until the bottoms are nicely browned, about 8 minutes.

3. Return the bacon to the skillet. Add the vinegar and maple syrup and toss again. Cook until the sauce is beginning to thicken and reduce, about 1 minute. Remove from the heat and serve directly from the skillet.

Scallion Cheddar Hash Brown Patties

Makes 8 patties

My earliest recollections of hash browns involve my grandparents whisking my sister and me to McDonald's for a secret breakfast any time they babysat. They always let me order an extra hash brown, which made the trip feel even more special. Plus, I'm pretty sure this core memory sparked my lifelong obsession with breakfast potatoes, from hash browns to home fries to tater tots and every crispy creation in between. These cheesy scallion hash brown patties are the ultimate combo of all my favorite breakfast potato flavors. Top one with a fried egg, and you've got yourself a complete, mouthwatering meal that'll make any breakfast (or dinner!) a hit.

Make Ahead: The cooked patties can be cooled and refrigerated in an airtight container up to 3 days; bring to room temperature before rewarming in a skillet.

⅓ cup all-purpose flour, plus more as needed

2 tablespoons cornstarch

1 tablespoon kosher salt

1 teaspoon freshly ground black pepper

1 teaspoon garlic powder

1 teaspoon onion powder

2 pounds russet potatoes, peeled and grated

2 large eggs, beaten

2 cups grated sharp cheddar cheese

8 scallions, thinly sliced

3 tablespoons extra-virgin olive oil, plus more as needed

Flaky salt, for serving

1. In a large bowl, whisk the flour, cornstarch, salt, pepper, garlic powder, and onion powder.

2. In a separate large bowl, wash and drain the grated potatoes a few times with hot water until the water is mostly clear. Set the potatoes in a clean kitchen towel and, over the sink, twist the towel tightly to squeeze out as much excess water as possible.

3. Add the potatoes to the flour mixture and stir to combine. Add the egg, cheese, and scallions and stir to combine; the mixture should be sticky but hold together. Add more flour, ½ tablespoon at a time, as needed.

4. Line a rimmed sheet pan with parchment paper. Divide and shape the potato mixture into 8 equal-size rectangular patties, about ¼ inch thick. Transfer to the freezer to chill for 30 minutes.

5. Heat the olive oil in a large nonstick skillet over medium heat until it shimmers. Working in batches, add the chilled patties and cook until golden brown and crisp, about 3 minutes per side. Transfer to paper towels to drain and sprinkle the tops with flaky salt. Add more oil to the skillet as needed. Serve the patties as soon as the last batch is finished.

Note
To keep the patties warm, line a second rimmed sheet pan with foil and set a wire rack on top. Place the prepared pan in the oven and preheat to 200°F. As you cook each batch, transfer to the wire rack in the oven to stay warm.

Diner Omelets *for a* Crowd

Serves 6

I might be walking on eggshells here, but I think a broccoli cheddar sausage omelet is the pinnacle of diner breakfast food. And I'm a diner girl through and through. Because we can't all be short-order cooks, this recipe allows you to have a bunch of omelets ready all at once, all in one pan, perfect for feeding a lot of hungry people. The cheese stays melty, the broccoli remains crisp, the sausage is juicy, and the eggs are wonderfully fluffy. You'll only have to shout "order up!" once for this big dish.

Make Ahead: Assemble the omelets, cover with cling wrap, and refrigerate up to 24 hours; bring to room temperature before finishing.

1 pound sweet or spicy Italian sausage, casings removed

1 medium head broccoli, cut into small florets

Kosher salt and freshly ground black pepper

3 tablespoons unsalted butter, cubed

18 large eggs

4 cups shredded cheddar cheese

1. Preheat the oven to 400°F.

2. In a 10-inch nonstick skillet, crumble the sausage into small pieces. Cook over medium heat until the fat is rendered and the sausage is browned, about 6 minutes. Add the broccoli, season with salt and pepper and cook, stirring occasionally, until it's bright green and crisp-tender, about 4 more minutes. Transfer the mixture to a large bowl and wipe out the skillet.

3. Melt 1 tablespoon of the butter in the same skillet over medium heat. In a small bowl, whisk 3 eggs with a generous pinch each of salt and pepper. Pour the eggs into the skillet and blanket with ⅓ cup of the cheese. Cover, and cook, undisturbed until the top is just set and the cheese is melted, 2 to 3 minutes. Slide the omelet onto a cutting board and let cool while repeating this process with 3 more eggs and another ⅓ cup cheese. While the second batch cooks, top the omelet on the cutting board with ⅔ cup of the sausage-broccoli mixture. Roll it up tightly and nestle it into a 9 × 13-inch baking dish, seam side down. Repeat the assembly line, melting more butter in the skillet after every other omelet, to make six rolled omelets in the baking dish. Blanket the top with the remaining 2 cups cheese.

4. Bake for about 8 minutes, until the cheese is melted and all the omelets are warmed through. Serve immediately.

DINER OMELETS
FOR A CROWD,
PAGE 98

Raisin Walnut Baked French Toast

Serves 8

It tastes like French toast, it feels like bread pudding, and you have no choice but to make it ahead? What more could you want! Packed with sweet raisins and crunchy walnuts, this baked French toast saves you from the agony of dipping and flipping slices while trying to be the hostess with the mostess. Instead, you get all the same joy in just one pan, hands off. My undying love for raisins persists, and, yes, you can leave them out—but I wouldn't be Grossy if I wasn't sneaking them in somewhere!

Make Ahead: The French toast can be assembled in the baking dish, covered with cling wrap, and refrigerated up to 12 hours before baking.

FRENCH TOAST

Nonstick cooking spray

1 (1-pound) loaf challah or brioche, cut into ¾-inch-thick slices

¼ cup raisins

¼ cup chopped walnuts

6 large eggs

½ cup packed light brown sugar

2 cups whole milk

1 cup heavy cream

1 tablespoon almond, vanilla, or rum extract

1 teaspoon ground cinnamon

½ teaspoon kosher salt

TOPPING

1 cup packed light brown sugar

½ cup (1 stick) unsalted butter, at room temperature

½ teaspoon kosher salt

½ teaspoon ground cinnamon

¼ cup raisins

¼ cup chopped walnuts

Powdered sugar, for serving

Pure maple syrup, warmed, for serving

1. **MAKE THE FRENCH TOAST:** Coat a 9 × 13-inch baking dish with nonstick spray. Add the bread in two rows, shingling the slices. Sprinkle the raisins and walnuts all around.

2. In a large bowl, whisk the eggs and brown sugar. Add the milk, heavy cream, almond extract, cinnamon, and salt and whisk again. Pour the mixture evenly over the bread. Cover the baking dish tightly with cling wrap and refrigerate for at least 4 hours or overnight.

3. Preheat the oven to 350°F. Remove the French toast from the fridge and uncover.

4. **MAKE THE TOPPING:** In a medium bowl, mash the brown sugar, butter, salt, and cinnamon. Add the raisins and walnuts to the sugar mixture and sprinkle it evenly over the French toast.

5. Bake for 40 to 45 minutes until the toast is golden brown and puffy. Let cool for 10 minutes in the dish. Dust with powdered sugar before serving big scoops with plenty of warm maple syrup on the side.

Blackberry Lemon Dutch Baby

Serves 4 to 6

I have to confess that I didn't encounter my first Dutch baby until well into adulthood. When I finally did, I was mesmerized—so chic, so refined, so delicate (basically, the opposite of me). I assumed only the finest pastry chefs in restaurant kitchens could pull it off. Surprise! They're pretty easy to make. These fluffy, oven-puffed pancakes are the perfect canvas for all kinds of toppings, from a simple dusting of powdered sugar to a pile of fresh fruit. My personal favorites are tangy blackberries mixed with tart lemon zest for an extra zing!

BLACKBERRY TOPPING

Zest and juice of 1 lemon

3 tablespoons sugar

1 pint fresh blackberries

DUTCH BABY

3 large eggs, at room temperature

¾ cup whole milk, at room temperature

¾ cup all-purpose flour

1 tablespoon sugar

½ teaspoon kosher salt

4 tablespoons (½ stick) unsalted butter, cubed

Powdered sugar, for serving

Pure maple syrup, warmed, for serving

1. Place a 10- or 12-inch cast-iron skillet in the oven and preheat to 425°F.

2. **MAKE THE TOPPING:** In a medium bowl, combine the lemon zest and sugar and use your fingers to pinch until fragrant and combined. Add the blackberries and use the back of a soup spoon to smash them into uneven pieces. Stir in the lemon juice.

3. **MAKE THE DUTCH BABY:** In a blender, blend the eggs on high until combined and bubbly, about 1 minute. Add the milk, flour, sugar, and salt. Blend for another minute on high, until thoroughly mixed into a smooth, runny batter.

4. Carefully remove the hot skillet from the oven and scatter the butter pieces around. Tilt to coat the skillet as the butter melts, then immediately pour in the batter. Transfer the skillet to the oven.

5. Bake, without opening the door, for 15 minutes, until the Dutch baby is golden brown, puffy, and climbing up the sides of the skillet. Seriously, do not peek. Remove from the oven and spoon the blackberry mixture over the top. Dust with powdered sugar and serve immediately with warm maple syrup alongside.

Sunrise Mom-osas

Makes 6 drinks

Name a more iconic duo than moms and a sunrise. Moms are up first, getting their day started, sipping on hot coffee, and enjoying the peace and quiet while the rest of the house is still fast asleep. Sunrise is peak Mom Time. When everyone finally wakes up, and food has magically appeared on the table, we know exactly who to thank. So let's make a toast to the moms who deserve a gorgeous drink any time of day—and this stunning mom-osa is just the thing. The layers make a beautiful sunrise ombré in the glass, and for a moment they can have both peace *and* quiet.

1 (52-ounce) bottle orange juice

1 (25.4-ounce) bottle sparkling apple cider

1 (12-ounce) bottle grenadine syrup

6 orange wheels, for serving

1. If you like, chill tall glasses or champagne flutes in the freezer for at least 1 hour.

2. Fill each glass halfway with orange juice. Add sparkling cider to fill each glass three-quarters of the way.

3. Working with one drink at a time, hold the bowl of a spoon upside down just above the surface of the drink and slowly pour the grenadine over the spoon, allowing the liquid to slide down the side into the drink, creating a layered effect. Garnish each drink with an orange wheel before serving.

Pumpkin *Spice* Up Your Life

Make THE Menu

● 2 DAYS BEFORE

Autumnal Cheese Ball: Make the cheese mixture and store in the fridge.

Radicchio, Gorgonzola & Pepita Salad: Make the dressing and store in the fridge.

● 1 DAY BEFORE

Roasted Squash with Crispy Chickpeas & Feta: Make the crispy chickpeas and store at room temperature.

Creamy Pumpkin Sauce: Make the sauce and store in the fridge.

Ginger Pumpkin Pie with Maple Whipped Cream: Make the pie without topping and store at room temperature.

● MORNING OF

Autumnal Cheese Ball: Make the pecans, assemble the cheese ball, and store in the fridge.

I GET IT—PUMPKIN SPICE HAS BECOME A CULTURAL CLICHÉ.
We either love it or we love to hate it. But I will stand alongside every
messy-bun-sporting and scarf-wielding girl to defend its honor to the
bitter end. Pumpkin spice is more than just a blend of seasonings, it's a
full-on lifestyle celebrating *my* favorite season: fall!

The first chill of fall means switching out the closet for cozy
sweaters, piling on blankets for marathon TV sessions, donning
wool socks for apple picking, and loudly announcing to anyone and
everyone, "Now *this* is my kind of weather."

As the days get shorter and the nights get longer, I crave the coziest
foods—the dishes you want to wrap yourself in and savor slowly.
Dinners by candlelight that stretch into the night, heavy tablecloths,
and a roaring fire are all on my mood board. The world may not need
pumpkin-spiced hair gel (that's real; look it up), but you definitely need
the recipes in this chapter for your ultimate pumpkin-spiced party to
embrace the (pumpkin) spice of life!

● **3 HOURS BEFORE**

Pumpkin Cider Braised Pork Shoulder: Braise the pork. Keep whole and cover to keep warm.

● **1 HOUR BEFORE**

Roasted Squash with Crispy Chickpeas & Feta: Marinate the shallots, cut the squash, and arrange on a sheet pan.

● **30 MINUTES BEFORE**

Roasted Squash with Crispy Chickpeas & Feta: Roast the squash and assemble the dish.

● **15 MINUTES BEFORE**

Radicchio, Gorgonzola & Pepita Salad: Assemble the salad.

Creamy Pumpkin Sauce: Reheat the sauce, boil the pasta, and toss together.

● **SERVING TIME**

Pumpkin Cider Braised Pork Shoulder: Slice or shred the pork and arrange on a platter.

Ginger Pumpkin Pie with Maple Whipped Cream: Make the topping and serve for dessert.

Autumnal Cheese Ball

Serves 8

Cheese balls are one of the greatest culinary inventions of all time. Just the idea of seeing one sitting at the center of an hors d'oeuvres spread makes me giddy. Decorated inside and out, this gob of goodness is meant to be scooped, spread, and shared with friends. With pumpkin puree and sage giving it that perfect autumnal outfit and maple-coated candied pecans adding the perfect crunch, this cheese ball is easy to fall in love with.

Make Ahead *The mixture can be refrigerated up to 48 hours. The finished cheese ball can be refrigerated up to 8 hours.*

CHEESE BALL

8 ounces cream cheese, cubed

8 ounces shredded mild cheddar cheese

¼ cup pumpkin puree

¼ cup fresh sage leaves

1 teaspoon pumpkin pie spice

PECANS

2 cups pecan halves

2 tablespoons pure maple syrup

1 teaspoon pumpkin pie spice

Crackers and sliced fruit, for serving

1. **MAKE THE CHEESE BALL:** In a food processor, combine the cream cheese, cheddar, pumpkin puree, sage, and pumpkin pie spice. Process, stopping to scrape down the sides as needed, until fully combined, about 3 minutes. Scrape the mixture into a small bowl, cover tightly with cling wrap, and refrigerate at least 4 hours or up to 48 hours

2. **MAKE THE PECANS:** In a medium skillet, arrange the pecans in an even layer. Cook over medium heat, tossing occasionally, until warm and fragrant, about 5 minutes. Remove from the heat and stir in the maple syrup and pumpkin pie spice. Let the mixture cool in the skillet to harden, about 10 minutes, then transfer to a cutting board and finely chop. Spread out the pecan pieces on a cutting board.

3. Remove the cheese mixture from the fridge. With damp hands, shape the cheese into a smooth, perfect sphere. Roll it over the pecans, gently pressing to adhere, until covered all over. Set on a serving plate and refrigerate until ready to serve with crackers and fruit.

Radicchio, Gorgonzola & Pepita Salad

Serves 6 to 8

Radicchio is the supermodel of salad greens: It's beautiful, bold, and sometimes a little bit bitter. It also pairs perfectly with smooth maple vinaigrette, creating a simple but spectacular salad. Radicchio's sturdy leaves can handle all the toppings you can throw at them, making it ideal for a fall harvest feast. Gorgonzola, the sweet Italian blue cheese, adds a creamy kick, while pepitas bring a nutty crunch and pears give it a soft sweetness. The colors of this salad are a true autumnal masterpiece, and I get lost in its beauty every time.

Make Ahead The vinaigrette can be refrigerated in an airtight container up to 1 week.

MAPLE VINAIGRETTE

½ cup balsamic vinegar

6 tablespoons pure maple syrup

1 tablespoon Dijon mustard

Kosher salt and freshly ground black pepper

½ cup extra-virgin olive oil

SALAD

2 Bartlett pears

Juice of 1 lemon

1 tablespoon extra-virgin olive oil

½ cup pepitas

Kosher salt

2 medium heads radicchio, quartered and cored, leaves separated

8 ounces Gorgonzola cheese, crumbled into large pieces

1. **MAKE THE VINAIGRETTE:** In a blender, combine the vinegar, maple syrup, Dijon, and a big pinch each of salt and pepper. Blend on low speed to combine, then, with the blender running, slowly pour in the olive oil. Stop blending as soon as the oil is fully incorporated.

2. **MAKE THE SALAD:** Core and thinly slice the pears and place them in a small bowl. Add the lemon juice and toss to coat.

3. In a small skillet, heat the olive oil over medium heat. When the oil is shimmering, add the pepitas and season with salt. Toss to coat the seeds in the oil and cook until just beginning to brown, 2 to 3 minutes. Use a slotted spoon to transfer the pepitas to a small bowl to cool.

4. Arrange the radicchio leaves on a serving platter. Scatter the Gorgonzola around the leaves. Drain the pear slices and arrange them around the radicchio and cheese, then sprinkle the pepitas over the top. Serve immediately with the dressing alongside.

Roasted Squash *with* Crispy Chickpeas & Feta

Serves 6 to 8

Is it even fall if there's not squash on the table? While I love a butternut as much as the next girl, this salad celebrates her less-famous sisters: delicata, acorn, and kabocha. All three have a dense and creamy texture and stunning orange flesh that looks gorgeous stacked on a platter. Roasted chickpeas add a crispy crunch, and a mixture of lightly pickled shallots, cooling mint, and salty feta will make you see squash in a whole new light.

Make Ahead The chickpeas can be cooled and stored at room temperature in an airtight container up to 24 hours.

3 medium shallots, sliced

½ cup apple cider vinegar

1 (15.5-ounce can) chickpeas, drained and rinsed

6 tablespoons extra-virgin olive oil

Kosher salt

2 medium delicata squash, cut into ½-inch-thick rounds and seeded (see Note)

1 medium acorn squash, halved lengthwise, seeded, and sliced into 6 wedges

1 medium kabocha squash, halved lengthwise, seeded, and sliced into 8 wedges

Cayenne pepper

2 teaspoons smoked paprika

8 ounces feta cheese, crumbled into large pieces

¼ cup loosely packed fresh mint leaves

Honey, for serving

1. Place the oven racks in the top (6 inches from the heat source) and center of the oven and preheat to 400°F.

2. **MAKE THE SHALLOTS:** In a small bowl, toss the shallots with the apple cider vinegar. Set aside to marinate.

3. **MAKE THE CRISPY CHICKPEAS:** Pat the chickpeas completely dry with paper towels, then spread them out on a rimmed sheet pan. Drizzle with 2 tablespoons of the olive oil, sprinkle with salt, and toss to coat. Spread out in a single layer.

4. **MAKE THE SQUASH:** On a second rimmed sheet pan, add all the squash and drizzle with the remaining 4 tablespoons olive oil, a good pinch of salt, and a light dusting of cayenne. Toss to coat, then arrange in a single layer. The squash can be all mixed up, it does not need to be organized by type.

5. Place the chickpeas on the top rack and the squash on the center rack of the oven. Roast for about 30 minutes, until the chickpeas are beginning to crisp and the squash is very tender. Remove the chickpeas, sprinkle the paprika over top, and shake the sheet pan to coat. Set aside to cool and finish crisping on the sheet pan. Turn on the broiler and move the squash to the top oven rack. Cook for 3 to 5 minutes, until nicely charred. Use tongs to pile the squash onto a serving platter.

6. Scatter the chickpeas over and around the squash. Drain the shallots and sprinkle them over the squash, along with the feta and mint. Drizzle a generous amount of honey over everything and finish with a couple pinches of cayenne before serving.

Note
If you want to keep your delicata rings intact like I do, use a dessert spoon to carefully pop out the seeds after slicing.

Pumpkin Cider Braised Pork Shoulder

Cold weather calls for long, slow-cooked meals, and pork shoulder is the perfect candidate—it just gets more tender the longer it cooks. This set-it-and-forget-it recipe combines sweet pumpkin cider—inspired by my sister, Diana, whose fridge is always stocked with pumpkin drinks in the fall—plus brown sugar and a ton of garlic and sage to let the pork sink into a deliciously sweet and savory sauce. The aromas from this slow roast are better than any scented candle, I guarantee it!

Serves 6 to 8

3 to 3½ pounds boneless pork shoulder

Kosher salt and freshly ground black pepper

¼ cup extra-virgin olive oil

2 (16-ounce) cans pumpkin cider, or 2 (12-ounce) bottles pumpkin ale

¼ cup packed dark brown sugar

2 medium red onions, halved and thinly sliced

10 garlic cloves, thinly sliced

2 bunches sage

1. Preheat the oven to 350°F.

2. Pat the pork dry with paper towels, then season generously with salt and pepper. In a large Dutch oven, heat the olive oil over medium heat. When the oil is shimmering, add the pork and cook until golden brown all over, about 5 minutes per side.

3. Pour in the pumpkin cider, then add the brown sugar, onions, garlic, sage, and I cup water. Bring to a simmer, then cover the pot. Transfer to the oven and bake for 2½ to 3 hours, flipping the pork halfway through, until the meat is falling apart and tender all the way through.

4. Use two forks to shred the pork into large pieces and let rest for 10 minutes. Skim as much fat as possible off the liquid in the pot, discarding it. Taste the remaining liquid for seasoning and add more salt and pepper as needed. Serve immediately.

Creamy Pumpkin Sauce

Serves 6 to 8

When I got my driver's license, I would borrow my parents' station wagon and drive thirty minutes to my favorite restaurant: The County Seat in downtown Litchfield, Connecticut. I couldn't get enough of their pumpkin pasta: a creamy, thick sauce blanketing tender, cheese-filled ravioli. Actually, this very dish might be the origin story of my obsession with pumpkin spice. Am I having a breakthrough? Maybe, so I had to make my own version to process. This smooth pumpkin sauce builds layers of flavor with garlic, thyme, and white wine, plus a little kick from red pepper flakes. Think of it as the autumnal sister to my famously thick vodka sawce.

Make Ahead *The sauce can be refrigerated in an airtight container up to 24 hours.*

Kosher salt

1 (20-ounce) package cheese ravioli

2 tablespoons extra-virgin olive oil

1 large white onion, diced

2 garlic cloves, minced

2 tablespoons fresh thyme leaves, plus more for serving

Red pepper flakes

1 cup dry white wine

1 (15-ounce) can pumpkin puree

½ teaspoon ground nutmeg, plus more as needed

½ cup heavy cream

Freshly grated Parmesan cheese, for serving

Freshly ground black pepper

1. Bring a large pot of salted water to a boil over high heat. Add the ravioli and cook until al dente according to the package directions. Reserve 1 cup of the pasta cooking water, then drain.

2. Meanwhile, heat the olive oil in a Dutch oven over medium heat. When the oil is shimmering, add the onion, garlic, thyme, and a pinch each of salt and pepper flakes. Cook, stirring occasionally, until the onion is soft, about 5 minutes. Pour in the wine and cook until slightly reduced, about 5 minutes more.

3. Transfer the mixture to a blender and add the pumpkin puree and nutmeg. Blend on high speed until smooth, about 1 minute. Pour the mixture back into the Dutch oven. Stir in the heavy cream and set over low heat to keep warm.

4. Add the ravioli and ¼ cup pasta cooking water and stir until the sauce is creamy and the ravioli are coated. Add a little bit more pasta cooking water as needed to make a smooth sauce.

5. Taste for seasoning and add more salt, pepper flakes, or nutmeg as needed, then transfer the pasta to a serving platter or bowl. Sprinkle with plenty of Parmesan, thyme leaves, and a few cracks of black pepper before serving.

Ginger Pumpkin Pie *with* Maple Whipped Cream

Serves 8

Hosting at my house upstate is the best part about my house upstate (did I mention I have a house upstate?), and I especially love collaborating with Gus on a menu. He brings a lot of his own traditions to the table, including an unforgettable pumpkin pie recipe he inherited from his mom, Cath, who uses gingersnaps in the crust. Like . . . say less. This twist on a classic pumpkin pie has become a staple in our autumnal rotation. When you finish baking it, you want the center of the pie to still have a little wobble—if it overbakes, the filling will split. When it's cooling, the residual heat will finish cooking that middle part all the way through, so don't have a pie panic!

Make Ahead The finished pie can be covered with cling wrap and stored at room temperature up to 3 days.

CRUST

4 cups gingersnap cookies
¼ cup packed dark brown sugar
1 teaspoon ground ginger
½ teaspoon kosher salt
1 large egg white
2 tablespoons unsalted butter, melted

FILLING

1 (15-ounce) can pumpkin puree
1 cup packed dark brown sugar
1½ teaspoons pumpkin pie spice
1 teaspoon kosher salt
1 cup heavy cream
2 large eggs
1 large egg yolk

TOPPING

1 cup heavy cream
2 tablespoons pure maple syrup

1. Preheat the oven to 350°F.

2. **MAKE THE CRUST:** In a food processor, combine the gingersnaps, brown sugar, ginger, and salt. Process into fine crumbs, about 2 minutes. Pour in the egg white and butter and process again until a crumbly dough forms, about 1 minute.

3. Press the dough along the bottom and up the sides of a 9-inch pie plate to make an even crust. Cover the crust with parchment and fill with pie weights or dried beans. Bake until just set, about 5 minutes. Let the crust cool completely, about 1 hour, then remove the weights and parchment.

4. Increase the oven temperature to 400°F.

5. **MAKE THE FILLING:** In a medium saucepan, whisk together the pumpkin puree, brown sugar, pumpkin pie spice, and salt. Cook over medium heat, whisking constantly, until thickened, about 5 minutes. Remove from the heat and let cool in the saucepan for about 5 minutes, then whisk in the cream. Add the eggs and yolk and whisk until fully combined.

6. Scrape the filling into the pie crust, smoothing out the top. Bake for 15 minutes, then reduce the oven temperature to 350°F. Bake for about 30 minutes, until the filling is mostly set but the center has some give when you wiggle the plate. Transfer to a wire rack to finish setting and cool completely, about 4 hours.

7. **JUST BEFORE SERVING, MAKE THE TOPPING:** In a medium bowl, whisk the heavy cream and maple syrup until soft peaks form. Slice and serve the pie with a dollop or two of whipped cream per piece.

Pumpkin CARVING Party

Grossy's Guide

When I'm hosting friends, I love a good activity. I think I might have been the arts-and-crafts counselor at a summer camp in another life. Now, tackling a puzzle with dessert or a round of Two Truths and a Lie over dinner are my old standbys. But when fall hits, I send out the dinner invite with a request that everyone BYOP (that's bring your own pumpkin). Then what, you ask? We carve! Here's how:

Let's Table This

If the weather is nice, pumpkin carving is the ideal outdoor activity because things can get a little messy. But indoors or out, cover your surface with newspaper or brown butcher paper, easily found at any craft supply store. Take it from this busy mom: Wadding up and recycling paper is much easier than scrubbing off pumpkin guts.

Sharp Thinking

I empty out my knife drawer, grab a few serving spoons, and gather up the scattered Sharpies from every junk drawer. For those who are a little knife shy, I pull out my metal cookie cutters and a rubber mallet so they can tap to cut designs out of the pumpkin. Don't waste your money on special kits and tools; everyday stuff is really all you need.

The Extra Mile

If you're really feeling like putting in the effort, you can find plenty of free pumpkin stencils online to print out. For those who are less interested in carving, set out paints and glitter for a more decorative pumpkin. And for the power tool lovers out there, yes, there is a drill attachment you can buy that will quickly scoop out the pumpkin guts. (Please don't tell Gus.)

The Secret Weapon

A thin layer of Vaseline on the cut edges of the pumpkins helps keep them from drying out and shriveling. This extra step will keep your pumpkins looking fresh and youthful for weeks! Works on faces, too, I think.

Light Them Up

Tea lights or votive candles are the classic accessory for a glowing pumpkin. I prefer LED candles, especially indoors, to avoid a fire hazard. Or really get creative and set out a few packs of glow sticks so your pumpkin party becomes a multicolored celebration.

● SAVE THE SEEDS

While everyone is carving their pumpkin, be sure the seeds are going in a large bowl. Fill the bowl with cold water and swirl to release the pulp. Skim the seeds from the surface and transfer to a colander. Rinse again and pick off any remaining pulp. Pat dry, arrange on a parchment paper–lined rimmed sheet pan, toss with a drizzle of neutral oil and any seasonings you want, and roast in a 300°F oven for 20 to 30 minutes, until they're golden brown and crispy. If you're me, this is your activity while the kids have fun carving.

Giving *Thanks*

Make THE *Menu*

● **2 DAYS BEFORE**

Grossy House Rolls with Chive Butter: Make the butter and store in the fridge.

Kevin's Roast Chicken over Stuffing: Season the chickens and store in the fridge.

● **1 DAY BEFORE**

Grossy House Rolls with Chive Butter: Complete the first rise, form the balls in the baking dish, and store in the fridge.

Don't Tell Your Nonna About This Lasagna: Assemble the lasagna and store in the fridge.

Spice Cake with Brown Sugar Frosting: Bake the cake layers and store at room temperature. Make the frosting and store in the fridge.

● **MORNING OF**

Spice Cake with Brown Sugar Frosting: Frost the cake and store in the fridge.

WHEN PEOPLE ASK ABOUT MY FAVORITE MEAL,

my answer is always Thanksgiving. The whole day has all my favorite things: family, endless comfort food, and eating dinner in the early afternoon so you can fill up your plate all over again later that night. It always makes me feel so cozy and content. The warm glow of the autumn sun filtering through the windows, the laughter echoing from every corner, and the aroma of things roasting make an atmosphere that's simply magical. If there's a better list of things to be grateful for, I do not know it.

Now that I have a house of my own, I get to play hostess and gather family *and* friends around my table. This menu isn't a strictly traditional Thanksgiving spread—with apologies to my family because we're skipping the antipasti platter that someone always brought but no one ever ate! It's my turn to make new memories and get creative with the dishes, adding my own twists to classic recipes.

Even if you gather weeks before or after the actual holiday, remember that hosting Thanksgiving is all about filling the table with things you love and then surrounding that table with people you love.

● **5 HOURS BEFORE**

Grossy House Rolls with Chive Butter: Remove the butter and rolls from the fridge to come to room temperature and rise.

● **3 HOURS BEFORE**

Grossy House Rolls with Chive Butter: Bake the rolls.

● **2 HOURS BEFORE**

(Spicy) Cranberry Relish: Make the relish and store in the fridge.

Roasted Carrot & Sweet Onion Galette: Bake the galette.

Don't Tell Your Nonna About This Lasagna: Bake the lasagna. Cover with foil to keep warm and reheat in the oven while baking the stuffing.

● **1 HOUR BEFORE**

Kevin's Roast Chicken over Stuffing: Roast the chickens and stuffing.

Spice Cake with Brown Sugar Frosting: Remove from the fridge to come to room temperature.

● **SERVING TIME**

Kevin's Roast Chicken over Stuffing: Carve the chickens and arrange over the stuffing.

Spice Cake with Brown Sugar Frosting: Serve the cake for dessert.

Grossy House Rolls *with* Chive Butter

Makes 16 rolls

I have a real soft spot for Parker House rolls: If they're on the menu, I'm ordering them. In that vein, these Grossy House Rolls are gorgeously pillowy and a little salty (kind of like me). They're perfectly sized so you can easily knock back four of them without batting an eye. Extra buttery and ridiculously easy to make, these rolls can go from being the first bite of your meal to sopping up every last drop on your plate. When you're at Grossy's House, we also use them for leftover sandwiches the next day—so you might want to make a double batch!

Make Ahead *The dough can be shaped and arranged in the baking dish, covered with cling wrap, and refrigerated up to 24 hours.*

ROLLS

I cup whole milk

2 tablespoons sugar

I (¼-ounce) packet active dry yeast

I large egg

I teaspoon kosher salt

3 cups all-purpose flour, plus more for dusting

4 tablespoons (½ stick) unsalted butter, at room temperature, plus 2 tablespoons, melted

Nonstick cooking spray

Flaky sea salt

CHIVE BUTTER

½ cup (I stick) unsalted butter, at room temperature

2 tablespoons sour cream

2 tablespoons thinly sliced fresh chives

½ teaspoon kosher salt

I. MAKE THE ROLLS: In a small saucepan, heat the milk over low heat until about 100°F, or warm to the touch but not hot. In the bowl of a stand mixer fitted with the dough hook, combine the warmed milk, sugar, and yeast. Let sit until the yeast is foamy and fragrant, about 5 minutes.

2. Add the egg, salt, and then the flour to the yeast mixture. Mix on low speed until combined, then increase the speed to medium. With the mixer running, add the butter, I tablespoon at a time, waiting until each addition is fully combined before adding the next. Continue to mix until the dough is soft, smooth, and pulling away from the bottom of the bowl, 8 to 10 minutes.

3. Lightly coat a large bowl with nonstick spray and transfer the dough to it. Cover tightly with cling wrap and set in a warm place to rise until doubled in size, about I hour.

4. Coat a 9 × 13-inch baking dish with nonstick spray. Lightly dust a work surface with flour. Punch the dough down in the bowl and turn it out onto the surface. Divide the dough into 16 equal pieces. Roll each piece into a ball, then place them in the prepared baking dish. Cover tightly with cling wrap and set in a warm place to rise until doubled in size, about I hour. Alternatively, refrigerate overnight and, the next day, set in a warm place to rise until doubled, about 2 hours.

5. MEANWHILE, MAKE THE CHIVE BUTTER: In a medium bowl, whisk together the butter, sour cream, chives, and salt. Set aside at room temperature until ready to use.

6. Place a rack in the lower third of the oven and preheat to 350°F.

7. Uncover the rolls. Brush the tops with the melted butter and generously sprinkle with flaky salt. Bake for 20 to 25 minutes, until golden brown on top. Let cool for at least 30 minutes before serving the rolls with the softened chive butter.

(Spicy) Cranberry Relish

Serves 8

Cranberry sauce is a family obsession, with at least three types showing up on our Thanksgiving table. My dad loves the classic jellied version from the can, complete with its signature plop; my sister boasts a homemade citrusy cranberry compote; and Aunt Chris always brings her famous pineapple and walnut cranberry Jell-O mold. Well, my cranberry relish adds a new twist to our cranberry canon. Taking cranberries to a savory, spicy place is a bold move that will impress your guests. If you're not a spicy girl, just swap out the cherry peppers for sweet peppers. A whole lime and orange (peel and all!) add unexpected flavor and texture—not bitter like you'd expect, but instead sweetly tart. Eat it by the spoonful or on top of everything else on your plate.

Make Ahead *The relish can be refrigerated in an airtight container up to 3 days.*

8 spicy cherry peppers or mini sweet peppers, stems removed

½ medium yellow onion, roughly chopped

1 navel orange, quartered

1 lime, quartered

12 ounces fresh cranberries, or 10 ounces frozen cranberries, thawed

1 cup sugar

2 tablespoons apple cider vinegar

1 teaspoon kosher salt

1. In a food processor, combine the peppers, onion, orange, and lime. Pulse 6 to 8 times, until roughly chopped. Add the cranberries, sugar, apple cider vinegar, and salt and pulse another 6 to 8 times until everything is broken down into a slightly chunky relish.

2. Transfer to a large bowl and cover tightly with cling wrap. Refrigerate for at least 2 hours before serving.

Roasted Carrot & Sweet Onion Galette

Sweet, roasted rainbow carrots and red onions painted across a canvas of tangy feta and framed in a golden, crispy puff pastry? Hang it in the MoMA! This flaky, golden galette looks like a masterpiece, but you don't have to be an artist to pull it off. Whether you make it ahead or pull it out of the oven just before your big meal, this vegetarian dish is surprisingly simple and brings a beautiful sense of drama to the table. Move over turkey, there's a new centerpiece in town!

Serves 8

2 pounds multicolored carrots, halved lengthwise

2 tablespoons extra-virgin olive oil

Kosher salt

8 ounces feta cheese

4 ounces goat cheese

2 tablespoons heavy cream

Leaves from 8 thyme sprigs

Leaves from 2 rosemary sprigs

I teaspoon freshly ground black pepper

All-purpose flour, for dusting

I puff pastry sheet, thawed

½ medium red onion, thinly sliced

FOR SERVING
Honey

Flaky salt

Freshly ground black pepper

I. Place racks in the center and lower third of the oven and preheat to 425°F.

2. On a rimmed sheet pan, toss the carrots with the olive oil and a few big pinches of salt. Arrange cut side down. Place the carrots on the center rack and roast for 20 minutes, until almost tender.

3. Meanwhile, break up the feta into a food processor and pulse to roughly crumble. Add the goat cheese, heavy cream, thyme, rosemary, and pepper. Process for about 2 minutes until smooth.

4. Lightly dust a work surface with flour. Roll out the puff pastry to a roughly 10 × 14-inch rectangle. Line a second rimmed sheet pan with parchment paper and transfer the pastry to it. Use a knife to score a ½-inch border on all sides and use a fork to dock the dough inside the border. Spread the cheese mixture onto the pastry, leaving a ½-inch border all around.

5. Arrange the roasted carrots on top of the cheese. Sprinkle the onion evenly over the carrots. Place the galette on the lower rack and bake for 15 to 20 minutes until the pastry is golden brown and puffed and the onions are beginning to brown.

6. Remove the galette from the oven and finish with a drizzle of honey, flaky salt, and pepper. Let cool on the sheet pan for at least 5 minutes before slicing and serving.

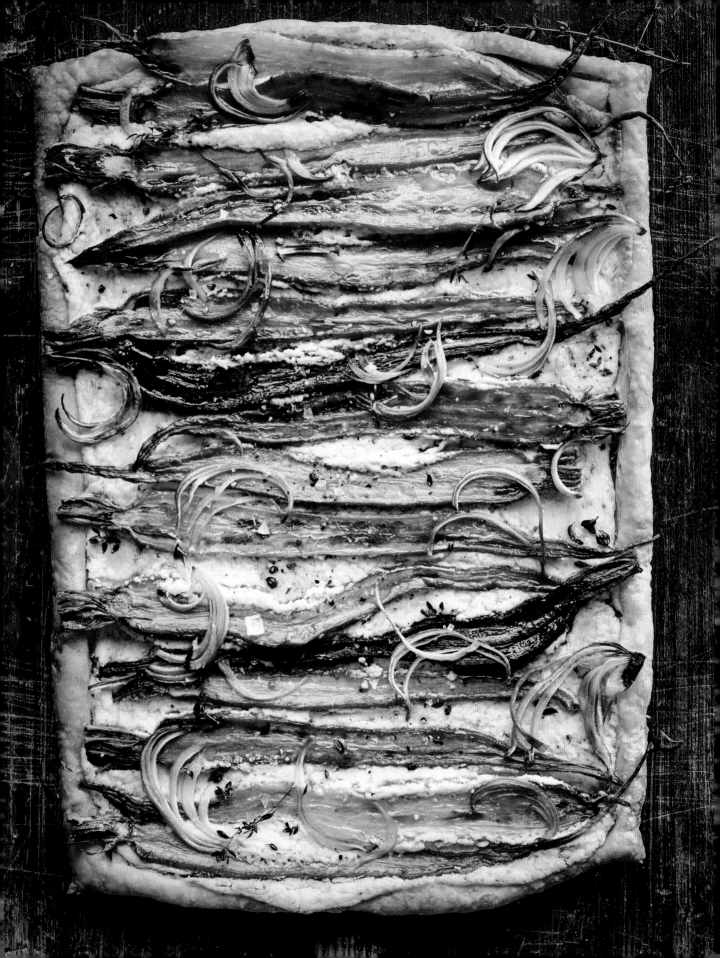

DON'T TELL YOUR NONNA ABOUT THIS LASAGNA, PAGE 136

Don't Tell Your Nonna About This Lasagna

Serves 8 to 10

This lasagna isn't the classic red sauce version Nonna is expecting to hit the table on Thanksgiving. Sorry, Nonna, we are creating new traditions here! Nothing makes me happier than a hearty, comforting lasagna, but I am a bit looser on what can be inside of it. Brussels sprouts, leeks, and Swiss chard are all Thanksgiving main characters, so when the cast appears together, tucked into the layers of this creamy, crispy, white sauce lasagna, it's the performance of a lifetime. An easy make-ahead, this dish is decadent enough to stand alone as a main course and is a hearty vegetarian option. I have a feeling even Nonna will approve, but I am not gonna be the one to tell her!

Make Ahead *The lasagna can be assembled in the baking dish, covered with foil, and refrigerated up to 3 days; bring to room temperature before baking.*

Nonstick cooking spray

BÉCHAMEL

½ cup (1 stick) unsalted butter

½ cup all-purpose flour

4 cups whole milk

1 tablespoon kosher salt

2 teaspoons freshly ground black pepper

1 teaspoon ground nutmeg

LASAGNA

1 (32-ounce) container whole-milk ricotta cheese

2 cups freshly grated Parmesan cheese, plus more for serving

2 tablespoons extra-virgin olive oil

1 pound Brussels sprouts, trimmed, halved, and thinly sliced

2 large leeks, halved, cleaned, and thinly sliced

1 bunch chard, stems removed and sliced into ribbons

4 garlic cloves, minced

Kosher salt and freshly ground black pepper

Red pepper flakes

2 (9-ounce) boxes no-boil lasagna noodles

1. Preheat the oven to 425°F. Coat a 9 × 13-inch baking dish with nonstick spray.

2. **MAKE THE BÉCHAMEL:** In a large saucepan, melt the butter over medium heat. Whisk in the flour and cook, stirring, until golden and fragrant, about 4 minutes. Whisk in the milk, about 1 cup at a time, being sure each addition is fully incorporated before adding the next. Add the salt, black pepper, and nutmeg, then cook, whisking often, until the béchamel thickens, about 10 minutes. Remove from the heat.

3. **MAKE THE LASAGNA:** In a medium bowl, stir together the ricotta and Parmesan.

4. In a large skillet, heat the olive oil over medium heat. When the oil is shimmering, add the Brussels sprouts, leeks, chard, and garlic and season with salt, black pepper, and pepper flakes. Cook, stirring occasionally, until the vegetables are vibrant and beginning to wilt, about 6 minutes.

5. Scoop a ladleful of béchamel into the bottom of the prepared baking dish. Build four layers of lasagna: Cover the béchamel with lasagna noodles, breaking them to fit as needed into an even layer. Ladle some béchamel on top. Scoop about one-third of the vegetables over the béchamel. Spoon a few dollops of the ricotta mixture on top of that. Repeat all these layers two more times, using up the vegetables and ricotta, but saving some béchamel. Add one final layer of noodles and gently press everything down. Pour ½ cup water over the lasagna, letting it seep into the pan. Spread the last of the béchamel over the noodles.

6. Cover the baking dish with foil and set on a rimmed sheet pan. Bake for 30 minutes. Remove the foil and bake for another 15 minutes, until the top is nicely browned and the inside is bubbling. Let the lasagna rest for 10 minutes. Dust the top with a little more Parmesan just before serving.

Kevin's Roast Chicken *over* Stuffing

Serves 6 to 8

In my experience, every friend group has that one person who has a solid, reliable roast chicken recipe. For me, that's my friend Kevin. For you, you will soon be that person! Instead of wrestling with a turkey on Thanksgiving, use Kevin's simple recipe to deliver a perfectly juicy, browned chicken with almost zero effort. It's my grounding force at the table, centering everything without stealing the show. Because we are giving thanks here, I slipped in the easiest stuffing you'll ever make. But this recipe is perfect for any gathering, any time of year. It's easy to love and endlessly reliable, just like Kevin.

Make Ahead The chicken can be seasoned and refrigerated up to 2 days; bring to room temperature before roasting.

CHICKEN

2 (3- to 4-pound) whole chickens

Kosher salt and freshly ground black pepper

4 tablespoons extra-virgin olive oil

1 medium red onion, quartered

1 lemon, quartered

1 head garlic, halved

Sage, thyme, and rosemary sprigs

STUFFING

1 large loaf sourdough bread or crusty bread, cut into 1-inch cubes

2 celery stalks, thinly sliced

2 shallots, thinly sliced

1 tablespoon finely chopped fresh sage leaves

1 tablespoon finely chopped fresh rosemary leaves

1 tablespoon fresh thyme leaves

1. Preheat the oven to 450°F.

2. **MAKE THE CHICKEN:** Pat the chickens dry with paper towels. Season very generously with salt and pepper all over and inside. Set the chickens on a rimmed sheet pan with space between them. Drizzle the olive oil over the birds, dividing evenly. Stuff each cavity with red onion, lemon, garlic, and herb sprigs. Bake for 30 minutes, then reduce the temperature to 400°F. Bake for 20 to 30 minutes more, depending on the size of the bird, until a thermometer inserted into the thickest part of the breast registers 160°F and the juices run clear. Transfer the chickens to a cutting board to rest; leave the oven on.

3. **MEANWHILE, MAKE THE STUFFING:** On the same rimmed sheet pan, toss the bread cubes in all the chicken juices. Evenly sprinkle the celery, shallots, sage, rosemary, and thyme over the bread. Bake for 10 minutes, until the bread is nicely toasted, then transfer to a serving platter.

4. Carve the chickens and set the pieces on top of the stuffing. Pour any juices from the cutting board over the top and serve immediately.

Note

To roast one chicken, follow the same instructions for seasoning and baking. But even when it's just Gus and me, I always roast two so we have leftovers in the fridge.

KEVIN'S ROAST CHICKEN OVER STUFFING, PAGE 137

Spice Cake *with* Brown Sugar Frosting

Serves 8 to 10

My brother-in-law's mother, Sheila, celebrates her birthday right around Thanksgiving, and her favorite dessert is spice cake. So on a table full of pies, I'm sure to have this cake ready and waiting for Sheila. With layers of moist cake spiced with all the best fall things—cinnamon, ginger, cloves, nutmeg—plus generous swirls of brown sugar buttercream frosting, this is the dessert we all deserve but didn't know we needed.

Make Ahead *The cake layers can be tightly wrapped with cling wrap and stored at room temperature up to 3 days. The frosting can be refrigerated in an airtight container up to 3 days.*

Nonstick cooking spray

CAKE

2 cups all-purpose flour

2 teaspoons baking powder

½ teaspoon baking soda

1 cup packed dark brown sugar

½ cup extra-virgin olive oil

½ cup applesauce

¼ cup unsulfured molasses

Zest of 1 orange

1 tablespoon ground cinnamon

1 tablespoon ground ginger

1 teaspoon kosher salt

1 teaspoon pure vanilla extract

½ teaspoon ground cloves

½ teaspoon ground nutmeg

2 large eggs

BROWN SUGAR FROSTING

1 (1-pound) box dark brown sugar

1 cup heavy cream

2 tablespoons unsulfured molasses

¼ teaspoon kosher salt

1 cup (2 sticks) unsalted butter, at room temperature

2 (1-pound) boxes powdered sugar

2 (8-ounce) packages cream cheese, very cold

1. Preheat the oven to 350°F. Coat two 9-inch round cake pans with nonstick spray. Line the bottoms with parchment rounds and coat those, too.

2. **MAKE THE CAKE:** In a medium bowl, whisk the flour, baking powder, and baking soda. In the bowl of a stand mixer fitted with the paddle attachment, beat the brown sugar, olive oil, applesauce, molasses, orange zest, cinnamon, ginger, salt, vanilla, cloves, and nutmeg on low speed until combined. Add the eggs, one at a time, beating each until fully combined before adding the next. Fold in half the flour mixture, then the rest. Divide the batter evenly between the prepared cake pans.

3. Bake the cakes for 30 to 40 minutes, until a tester inserted into the center of the cake comes out clean. Let cool completely in the pans, about 2 hours.

4. **MEANWHILE, MAKE THE FROSTING:** In a stand mixer fitted with the whisk attachment, beat the brown sugar, heavy cream, molasses, and salt on medium speed until combined, about 1 minute. Scrape down the sides and along the bottom of the bowl, then beat on high speed until the sugar is mostly dissolved, about 2 minutes. Add the butter and beat on medium until just combined, about 1 minute. Add half the powdered sugar and beat on low until combined, then repeat with the remainder. With the mixer running on low, break up the cream cheese into pieces and drop them into the bowl. Increase the speed to medium and beat until light and fluffy, about 3 minutes. Refrigerate in the bowl to set for at least 1 hour, bringing to room temperature for 5 minutes before using.

5. Remove the cakes from the pans and discard the parchment. Slice the tops off each cake so they're flat. Set one of the cake layers cut side up on a cake stand or serving plate. Spread about 1 cup of the frosting over the top of the cake, then place the other cake layer cut side down on top. Spread a thin layer of frosting over the top and sides of the cake and chill in the fridge for 30 minutes to set.

6. Spread the remaining frosting over the top and sides of the cake. Chill for another 30 minutes to set. Serve cold or bring to room temperature.

Grossy's Holiday Cookie Party

Grossy's Guide: **THE HOLIDAY COOKIE PARTY 144**

Make THE *Menu*

● **3 DAYS BEFORE**

Hot Chocolate with All the Fixings: Prepare the hot chocolate mix and store at room temperature.

Pignoli Cookies: Prepare the dough and store in the fridge.

Peppermint Pattie Cookies: Prepare the dough and store in the fridge.

Gingerbears: Prepare the dough and store in the fridge.

● **2 DAYS BEFORE**

Pignoli Cookies: Bake the cookies, cool, and store at room temperature.

Peppermint Pattie Cookies: Bake the cookies, cool, and store at room temperature.

Gingerbears: Bake the cookies, cool, and store at room temperature.

ITALIAN AMERICAN FAMILIES HAVE A UNIQUE TRADITION when it comes to holiday cookie exchanges. Everyone makes their own version of the exact same cookie, and, naturally, everyone insists theirs is the best. It's a delicious hysteria, and I absolutely love it. Holiday cookies have been a part of my life for as long as I can remember, and as a kid I'd joyfully sneak treats from the cookie tin that somehow stayed full the entire holiday season.

It was only natural that as an adult I started hosting my own holiday cookie party, which is, without contest, my favorite day of the year. I like to think I'm famous for many things, but this is the one thing I might actually be famous for. My holiday cookie party has grown from a small gathering in my West Village studio apartment to a major event happening in your homes across the country!

The true beauty of any cookie party is in the mingling and the storytelling. Every cookie and every baker has a story to tell, and I love seeing them all come out at the party. That's why store-bought cookies are absolutely banned! The whole point is sharing the love and joy of homemade cookies and the memories that come with them.

● **1 DAY BEFORE**

Spritz Cookies: Bake the cookies, cool, and store at room temperature.

Snowballs: Bake the cookies, roll in powdered sugar, and store at room temperature.

● **MORNING OF**

Salty Peanut Butter Toffee Bark: Make the bark and store in the fridge.

Spritz Cookies: Fill with jam, dip in chocolate, and finish with sprinkles.

Gingerbears: Make the icing and decorate.

● **30 MINUTES BEFORE**

Hot Chocolate with All the Fixings: Whisk in the milk and heat up.

Arrange all your cookies.

Grossy's Guide THE *Holiday* COOKIE PARTY

My annual holiday cookie party has become my signature event, and I look forward to it all year. What started as a small gathering in my West Village apartment has now gone on a world tour . . . literally. Guests come and go throughout the afternoon, the cookie table is constantly losing and gaining piles of cookies, and everyone loves to talk about who made what and share their story behind each cookie. If you want to jump on the bandwagon, here's everything you need to know to host a holiday cookie party.

SET THE *Time*

My party is an open house in the afternoon, because the only refreshments are cookies and drinks. I give a time range between lunch and dinner, so everyone can roll in and out as they please, and no one is expecting a full buffet of anything other than cookies. Any time works, but I think this style works best.

SET THE *Mood*

Turn up the holiday music and get the yule log roaring on the TV. I like to keep the focus on the cookies, so I go light on decorations, but if you feel like hanging up some twinkle lights or a little garland, go for it. Anything that starts to get you in the spirit is the right move.

SET THE *Menu*

There is no cookie party without the cookies! As the host, I always bake a few different holiday cookies so that the table immediately feels abundant. Holiday cookies are easy to make ahead and store, so you can easily get your work out of the way before the party. Be sure your

guests know their baking is what makes the party! I famously do not allow store-bought cookies at my holiday cookie party, because to me it's all about the beauty of my friends expressing themselves. But it's your party and you're welcome to break that rule if you want.

SET THE *Bar*

I tell guests who are not bakers to bring something festive for the bar! Some of my friends even get ambitious with a big-batch holiday cocktail. I set up a drinks station in the kitchen with stacks of cups and plenty of ice on hand. And because I firmly believe where there are

holiday cookies, there must be hot chocolate, I have warm hot chocolate on hand throughout the party (see page 146)!

SET THE *Table*

When you're doing this Grossy style, the table *is* the party. Clear off the largest table you own and call in backup from the folding tables in the basement if you need to. Cover the entire surface with a large roll of brown butcher paper, which is available at any craft supply store. I set out a few piles of small plates and cocktail napkins so everyone can snack on cookies during the party. When your guests arrive, ask them to arrange their cookies on the paper in neat little piles. Lay out Sharpies so each person can write their name, their cookie, and any allergens. (I also like everyone to include their Insta handle so they can tag one another.)

SET FOR *Later*

Store any leftover cookies in an airtight container (with a slice of bread!) at room temperature for up to 3 days. But I always put out a stack of brown paper lunch bags and encourage everyone to pack up a stash to go. Who doesn't love leaving a party with a goody bag?

● THE COOKIE DECORATING TABLE

Because I am a Pinterest Mom who loves a craft project (especially an edible one!), I always set a small cookie decorating table in a separate area of the party. Any kids or kids at heart immediately gravitate here. I like to bake a few batches of blank cookies (like my Gingerbears, page 154) and set out tubes of frosting, sprinkles, and edible decorations! Butter knives, spoons, and toothpicks are all you need for tools. A stack of paper towels is a must. Do yourself a favor and cover this table with butcher paper too because it can get pretty messy. This is an optional upgrade to your party, but one I highly recommend.

Hot Chocolate *with* All the Fixings

Makes 10 drinks

There was my cookie party, and then there was my cookie party *after* I acquired a hot chocolate machine. It warms, stirs, and dispenses perfect cups of hot chocolate, and it's so perfect I could cry. Next to the machine, I set out bowls of mini marshmallows, peppermint sticks, and bottles of liqueur for anyone who wants a little spike in their drink. Since not everyone has a hot chocolate machine on hand, this chocolaty, marshmallowy, minty mix works perfectly in a Dutch oven on the stove. And while any milk substitutes will work for a versatile and delicious drink, the mini marshmallows are not optional.

Make Ahead The hot chocolate mix can be stored in an airtight container at room temperature up to 2 months.

2 cups powdered sugar

1 cup unsweetened cocoa powder

2 teaspoons kosher salt

2 cups mini marshmallows, plus more for serving

1 cup semisweet chocolate chips

1 cup crushed peppermint candies

10 cups whole milk or any milk of your choice

1. In a large bowl, whisk together the powdered sugar, cocoa powder, and salt. Stir in the mini marshmallows, chocolate chips, and peppermint candies until well combined.

2. To make one large batch: In a large Dutch oven, bring the milk to a simmer over medium heat. Add the mix and whisk until completely combined and melted, about 2 minutes. Reduce the heat to low to keep warm while serving.

3. Serve with more mini marshmallows floating atop each mug.

Note:

To make individual mugs: Scoop ½ cup of mix into a mug and add 1 cup of warmed milk. Stir until the mixture melts, about 1 minute, before enjoying.

SNOWBALLS

GINGER BEARS

PIGNOLI
COOKIES

SALTY PEANUT BUTTER
TOFFEE BARK

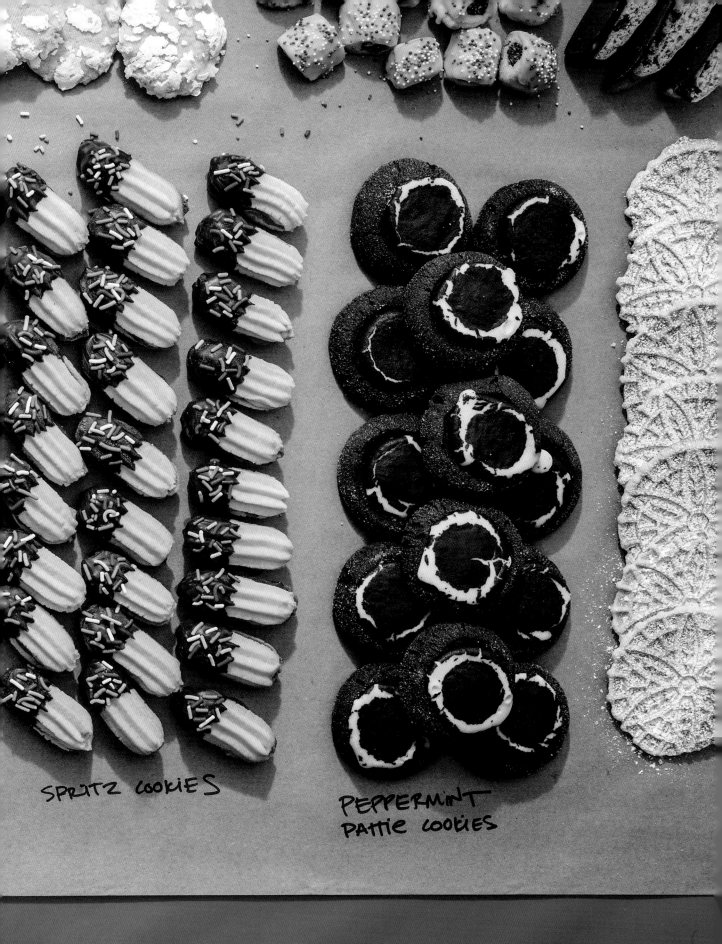

SPRITZ COOKIES

PEPPERMINT
PATTIE COOKIES

Pignoli Cookies

Makes 50 cookies

Pignoli cookies are the royalty of Italian sweets, gracing every Maria's holiday cookie tray with their presence. These beauties, encrusted in toasty pine nuts on the outside, are known for next-level chewiness on the inside. You'll probably notice pignoli (those are pine nuts, for the unacquainted) and almond paste aren't the cheapest ingredients I've ever had you use . . . but trust me, they're worth every penny. Bite into these and feel like the queen you are!

Make Ahead *The pignoli dough can be tightly wrapped with cling wrap and refrigerated up to 3 days or frozen up to 1 month, then thawed overnight in the fridge.*

24 ounces almond paste, refrigerated

1½ cups granulated sugar

1 cup powdered sugar

2 large egg whites

16 ounces pine nuts

1. Preheat the oven to 350°F. Line a rimmed sheet pan (or two, or three) with parchment paper.

2. In the bowl of a stand mixer fitted with the paddle attachment, combine the almond paste, granulated sugar, powdered sugar, and egg whites. Beat on medium speed until just combined into a sticky dough, about 2 minutes.

3. Pour the pine nuts into a small bowl. Scoop up 1 tablespoon of dough, roll into a ball, then roll through the pine nuts, pressing to adhere. Set on the prepared sheet pans. Repeat with the remaining dough, spacing them 1 inch apart.

4. Bake for 15 to 20 minutes, until the cookies are golden brown. Let the cookies cool completely before serving.

Salty Peanut Butter Toffee Bark

Makes about 24 pieces

If you're lucky, the holiday season means a never-ending parade of sweet treats marching through your home. One standout memory from my childhood is my mom's coworker, Diane, and her famous chocolate toffee bark. She'd deliver a huge tin of it, and it would vanish in no time. A jar of peanut butter was basically my security blanket when I was little (and maybe still is?), and I discovered early on that adding a dollop of peanut butter to her perfect bark was an absolute level-up. This updated chocolate peanut butter bark combines everything I love into one delicious bite.

1½ sleeves saltine crackers (about 54 crackers)

1½ cups packed dark brown sugar

1 cup (2 sticks) unsalted butter

½ teaspoon kosher salt

1 (12-ounce) bag semisweet chocolate chips

1 cup smooth peanut butter

1 cup chopped roasted, salted peanuts

Flaky salt, for serving

1. Preheat the oven to 350°F. Line a rimmed sheet pan with foil and place a piece of parchment on top of that.

2. Arrange the saltines along the bottom of the prepared sheet pan, breaking the crackers as needed to create a single layer.

3. In a medium saucepan, combine the brown sugar, butter, and salt. Cook over medium heat, whisking, until the butter is melted and the sugar begins to dissolve, about 2 minutes. Simmer, whisking constantly, until thick and foamy, about 3 minutes. Pour the toffee over the crackers, then use an offset spatula to spread it evenly.

4. Bake the crackers for about 15 minutes until the toffee is slightly deeper brown and bubbling all over. Remove from the oven and scatter the chocolate chips evenly over the top. Drop tablespoonfuls of the peanut butter across the surface. Let the bark sit for a minute or two, until the chocolate and peanut butter begin to melt, then spread and swirl both evenly over the top of the crackers. Immediately sprinkle the peanuts over the surface and finish with a few pinches of flaky salt.

5. Place the sheet pan in the fridge or freezer to set, about 30 minutes. Cut or break into about 24 pieces before serving.

Peppermint Pattie Cookies

Makes 18 cookies

One of my favorite holiday cookies is peanut butter blossoms, which, for the uninitiated are soft peanut butter cookies with Hershey's Kisses in the center. I've always wondered about other cookie-candy couples . . . How did they meet? Did their publicists set them up? Are they really in love? Enter our newest couple: the York Peppermint Pattie and chocolate cookie! Imagine a chewy, chocolaty cookie with a peppermint pattie plopped in the middle. As they bake, the chocolate coating on the patties cracks, revealing all their secrets via streaks of the chewy, minty center. This duo is fresh and festive and is a brand-new addition to my cookie gossip column . . . I mean, cookie table.

Make Ahead *The cookie dough can be tightly wrapped with cling wrap and refrigerated up to 3 days or frozen up to 1 month, then thawed overnight in the fridge; bring to room temperature before scooping.*

½ cup granulated sugar

1¾ cups all-purpose flour

¾ cup unsweetened cocoa powder

1 teaspoon baking soda

1 teaspoon kosher salt

1 cup packed dark brown sugar

¾ cup (1½ sticks) unsalted butter, melted and cooled

2 large eggs

1 tablespoon pure mint extract

18 York Peppermint Patties

1. Preheat the oven to 350°F. Line a rimmed sheet pan (or two) with parchment paper.

2. Place the granulated sugar in a small bowl. In a medium bowl, whisk together the flour, cocoa powder, baking soda, and salt.

3. In a large bowl, whisk the brown sugar and melted butter. Add the eggs and mint extract and whisk until incorporated. Add the flour mixture and mix until no streaks remain.

4. Scoop up a rounded 2 tablespoons of dough and roll it into a ball. Roll through the sugar to coat all over. Place on the prepared sheet pan and repeat with the remaining dough, spacing the balls 3 inches apart. (You'll need to work in batches or use a second sheet pan.) Press a Peppermint Pattie into the center of each ball, flattening it into a roughly 2-inch circle. Sprinkle the perimeter of each cookie with another pinch of sugar, then bake for about 12 minutes, until the edges are just starting to set and the candy is cracked. Let the cookies cool completely on the sheet pan.

Spritz Cookies

Makes 34 sandwich cookies

This cookie has nothing to do with the bubbly, orange, drinkable spritz you think it might—in fact, that's not even close! Spritz cookies are iconic staples of Italian American bakeries: two soft, buttery cookies sandwiching a strip of jam, then dipped in chocolate and covered in rainbow sprinkles. They just beg to be served with a cup of coffee and steaming-hot gossip. Making these at home is a little bit of a process, and requires a piping bag with a star tip, but it's not hard! Plus, it's a perfect reason to gather up friends and family to make a cookie production line.

Make Ahead *The baked cookies can be stored in an airtight container at room temperature up to 24 hours.*

I cup (2 sticks) unsalted butter, at room temperature

¾ cup sugar

2 large egg yolks

I teaspoon pure vanilla extract

I teaspoon kosher salt

½ teaspoon baking powder

2 cups all-purpose flour

½ cup apricot or seedless raspberry jam

I (10-ounce) bag semisweet chocolate chips

½ cup rainbow sprinkles

1. Preheat the oven to 350°F. Line a rimmed sheet pan (or two, or three) with parchment paper.

2. In a stand mixer fitted with the paddle attachment, beat the butter and sugar on medium speed until light and fluffy. Scrape down the sides of the bowl, then add the egg yolks, vanilla, salt, and baking powder and beat on medium speed to combine. Add the flour and beat on low until almost incorporated. Scrape down the sides and bottom of the bowl and finish folding in the flour by hand.

3. Fit a piping bag with a ½-inch star tip. Scrape the dough into the piping bag. On one of the prepared sheet pans, pipe the dough into 2-inch strips, spacing them 2 inches apart. Bake for about 10 minutes, until the edges are golden brown. Pipe the next sheet pan while each one bakes. Let the cookies cool completely on the sheet pans.

4. Scoop the jam into a piping bag fitted with a small round tip. Pair up cookies of similar sizes. Pipe about ½ teaspoon jam onto the flat side of one cookie, then gently press its partner on top to make sandwiches.

5. In a small saucepan, bring 2 inches of water to a boil over high heat. Set a medium bowl on top of the saucepan, being sure the bowl doesn't touch the water. Pour the chocolate chips into the bowl and reduce the heat to low. Cook, stirring occasionally, until the chocolate is melted, about 3 minutes. Turn the heat off, but leave the bowl on the saucepan to keep the chocolate warm.

6. Dip one side of each sandwiched cookie into the chocolate, about a third of the way up. Let the excess drip off, then finish with a few pinches of sprinkles all over the chocolate. Place the dipped cookies back on the parchment to set.

Gingerbears

Makes 24 cookies or more

Sure, you've heard of a gingerbread man—now, I'm pleased to introduce you to my friend, the gingerbear: the holiday version of my official mascot. These cookies, delicious on their own, are also the perfect spicy, chewy, and festive canvas for all the decorators out there. If bears aren't your thing, try stars, round ornaments, or whatever cookie cutter shape you have on hand! When I'm hosting my cookie party, I like to make an extra batch and set up a decorating table (see page 144), so my friends can enjoy a moment of self-expression. Their masterpieces are always one of my favorite parts of the party.

Make Ahead The cookie dough can be tightly wrapped with cling wrap and refrigerated up to 3 days or frozen up to 1 month, then thawed in the fridge.

COOKIES

3½ cups all-purpose flour, plus more for rolling

I tablespoon ground ginger

2 teaspoons ground cinnamon

I teaspoon baking soda

I teaspoon kosher salt

¼ teaspoon ground nutmeg

¼ teaspoon ground cloves

¼ teaspoon freshly ground black pepper

I cup packed dark brown sugar

½ cup (I stick) unsalted butter, at room temperature

½ cup unsulfured molasses

I large egg

2 tablespoons whole milk

I teaspoon pure vanilla extract

ICING

I (I-pound) box powdered sugar (3½ cups)

3 tablespoons whole milk, plus more as needed

¼ teaspoon pure vanilla, almond, rum, or maple extract

Food coloring (optional)

I. **MAKE THE COOKIES:** In a medium bowl, whisk together the flour, ginger, cinnamon, baking soda, salt, nutmeg, cloves, and pepper.

2. In the bowl of a stand mixer fitted with the paddle attachment, beat the brown sugar, butter, and molasses on high speed until combined and fluffy, about 2 minutes. Add the egg, milk, and vanilla and beat on high speed until incorporated. Add the flour mixture and beat on low until no streaks remain. The dough will be dense and slightly sticky.

3. Remove the dough from the bowl, pat together, and wrap tightly with cling wrap. Refrigerate overnight or up to 3 days.

4. Preheat the oven to 350°F. Line a rimmed sheet pan (or two, or three) with parchment paper.

5. Generously flour a work surface. Cut the dough in half; rewrap one half and return it to the fridge. Place the other half on the work surface and dust the top with flour. Roll out the dough to ¼-inch thickness. Use a cookie cutter to cut out shapes, placing them on the prepared sheet pan. Gather the scraps, reroll the dough, and continue cutting out shapes until you can't anymore!

6. Bake for about 8 minutes, until the cookies are puffed and just barely set on the edges. Let the cookies cool on the sheet pan for 5 minutes, then transfer to a wire rack to cool completely.

7. Remove the other half of the dough from the fridge and repeat the process.

8. **MEANWHILE, MAKE THE ICING:** In a large bowl, whisk the powdered sugar, milk, and vanilla until a thick frosting forms. Add more milk, I tablespoon at a time, as needed. If desired, divide the icing into separate bowls and add food coloring to make different colors. Transfer the icing to a disposable piping bag and snip ⅛ inch off the end.

9. Ice the cookies and add any decorations (see page I44). Let the decorated cookies sit for IO minutes to dry.

Snowballs

Makes 32 cookies

My Grandma Katherine made these every year for the holidays. She called them Butterballs, and when I had to pick one cookie off her holiday cookie tray to eat first, these were always it! These tender, buttery delights are packed with nuts and rolled through powdered sugar while they're still hot for an extra thick, irresistible coating. They just melt in your mouth with every bite. They're known by many names—Mexican Wedding Cookies, Russian Tea Cakes, Italian Wedding Cookies—and I like to call them Snowballs, thanks to their adorable powdery appearance.

1 cup (2 sticks) unsalted butter, at room temperature

1½ cups powdered sugar

2¼ cups all-purpose flour

¾ cups finely chopped raw almonds, pecans, and/or walnuts

1 teaspoon pure vanilla extract

1. Preheat the oven to 400°F. Line a rimmed sheet pan (or two, or three) with parchment paper.

2. In a stand mixer fitted with the paddle attachment, beat the butter and ½ cup of the powdered sugar on medium speed until combined. Add the flour, nuts, and vanilla and beat on low until no streaks remain.

3. Scoop up 1 rounded tablespoon of the dough and roll it into a ball. Place on the prepared sheet pan, spacing them 1 inch apart. (You'll need to work in batches or use more sheet pans.) Bake for about 10 minutes, until just barely set and the tops have started to crack.

4. Let the cookies cool for about 5 minutes on the sheet pan, just until cool enough to handle. Pour the remaining 1 cup powdered sugar into a small bowl. One at a time, roll the cookies through the powdered sugar to coat, then return to the sheet pan to cool completely.

Fishing for Compliments

Make THE Menu

● **1 DAY BEFORE**

Baccalà Balls: Soak the cod in cold water, changing the water every 8 hours.

Crispy Artichokes & Marinated Butter Beans: Combine the marinade and butter beans and store in the fridge.

Warm Farro Salad with Dried Fruit: Prepare the farro salad and store in the fridge.

Insalata di Frutti di Mare: Prepare the seafood salad and store in the fridge.

Roast Salmon with Smashed Olives: Salt the salmon and store in the fridge.

● **MORNING OF**

Baccalà Balls: Make the mixture and store in the fridge.

ANY TIME AN ITALIAN AMERICAN PUTS FOOD ON THE TABLE, they're fishing for compliments—but that's especially true when fish is the actual star of the show. Growing up in an Italian Catholic family meant a lot of fish-centered holidays, especially the iconic Feast of the Seven Fishes on Christmas Eve. Fridays and certain holidays were also strictly meat-free, so being a (former) good Catholic school girl, I'm always looking for new ways to serve seafood that keeps everyone excited.

This menu blows a fresh sea breeze on your own feast, with a few modern twists on beloved classics, plus hearty sides that keep the boat afloat. It's like a throwback with a makeover—classic flavors that still manage to keep you on your toes. But why relegate these goodies to Christmas Eve? They're perfect for any occasion when you want to impress with your seafood savvy, from elegant dinners to casual get-togethers. You'll be reeling in the compliments!

● **1 HOUR BEFORE**

Baccalà Balls: Shape and cook the cod balls. Keep warm in the oven.

Crispy Artichokes & Marinated Butter Beans: Cook the artichokes and assemble.

Warm Farro Salad with Dried Fruit: Remove from the fridge to come to room temperature.

● **30 MINUTES BEFORE**

Scallops over Angel Hair with Lemon & Tarragon: Cook the scallops, boil the pasta, and assemble.

Roast Salmon with Smashed Olives: Roast the salmon and spoon on the olive dressing.

● **SERVING TIME**

Insalata di Frutti di Mare: Serve cold.

Baccalà Balls

Serves 6 to 8

For me, it just doesn't feel like Christmas until the baccalà balls hit the table, fresh out of the fryer. Baccalà, or salted cod, is the star of this crispy, delicious appetizer. My mom and Aunt Chris, the queens of the Portuguese side of my family, keep the fryer hot and the tradition alive, but Italians have something similar around Christmas, too, so all sides of the family are satisfied. Mom says "*bolinhos de bacalhau*"; Dad says "*frittelle di baccalà*"; I just say "more please!"

Make Ahead: The baccalà mixture can be covered with cling wrap and refrigerated up to 24 hours.

10 ounces salted cod

1 pound russet potatoes

1 small white onion, finely chopped

2 tablespoons finely chopped fresh parsley

Zest and juice of 2 lemons

2 large eggs

2 quarts neutral oil

Lemon wedges, for serving

Flaky salt, for serving

1. Place the cod in a medium bowl and cover with cold water. Set aside to soak at room temperature for 24 hours, draining and refreshing the water every 8 hours or so. Drain the soaked cod and set aside.

2. Place the potatoes in a large saucepan. Cover with water and set over high heat. Bring the water to a boil, then cook until the potatoes are knife tender, about 20 minutes. Drain and let cool slightly.

3. Place the cod in the same pan from the potatoes. Cover with water and set over medium heat. Bring the water to a boil, then reduce the heat to low, cover, and cook until the cod is flaky, about 20 minutes.

4. Meanwhile, when the potatoes are cool enough to handle, peel them, then place in a large bowl. Lightly mash to break apart.

5. Drain the cod and add to the bowl with the potatoes. Continue mashing until the potatoes and cod are broken down. Add the onion, parsley, lemon zest and juice, and eggs and stir into a stiff mixture. (Your spoon should be able to stand up in it.) Cover the bowl tightly with cling wrap and refrigerate for at least 1 hour or up to 24 hours.

6. Meanwhile, fit a large Dutch oven with a thermometer, then add the oil. Heat over medium heat to 375°F. Scoop and shape the cod mixture into egg-shaped balls; you should have about 14.

7. Add about half the cod balls to the oil and cook until deeply golden brown, 5 to 7 minutes. Transfer to paper towels to drain. Repeat with the remaining cod, allowing the oil to return to 375°F first.

8. Arrange the fried balls on a serving plate with plenty of lemon wedges for squeezing and a bowl of flaky sea salt for sprinkling. Serve immediately.

Crispy Artichokes & Marinated Butter Beans

Serves 6 to 8

In his heyday, Bimpy was always first in line at ShopRite's bi-annual Can Can Sale. We joked that he stocked up on more canned food than he'd ever need, but at least he'd have enough to survive the apocalypse. I am pleased to announce that the apocalypse has yet to happen (I think?) and he's still working through his supply. Forever a disciple of the School of Bimpy, unsurprisingly, I love cooking with canned food. With a little effort anything can feel elevated, like this quick marinade of canned butter beans in herby oil and a sizzle of canned artichoke hearts in the skillet. Your pantry staples have never looked this good!

Make Ahead: The butter beans can marinate refrigerated in an airtight container up to 24 hours.

½ cup plus ⅓ cup extra-virgin olive oil, plus more as needed

¼ cup roughly chopped fresh basil

¼ cup roughly chopped fresh mint, plus more for serving

4 garlic cloves, grated

Kosher salt

½ teaspoon freshly ground black pepper

¼ teaspoon red pepper flakes, plus more for serving

1 (15.5-ounce) can butter beans, drained and rinsed

2 (14-ounce) cans quartered artichoke hearts, drained

1 (17.6-ounce) container plain full-fat Greek yogurt

Lemon wedges, for serving

1. In a small bowl, whisk together ½ cup of the olive oil with the basil, mint, garlic, ½ teaspoon salt, black pepper, and pepper flakes. Add the butter beans, stir to coat, and set aside to marinate.

2. In a large skillet, heat the remaining ⅓ cup olive oil over medium-high heat. Pat the artichokes completely dry with paper towels and season with salt. When the oil shimmers, add half the artichokes in an even layer. Cook until charred on the bottom, about 6 minutes, then flip. Cook until the other side is charred and the artichokes are crispy, another 6 minutes or so. Transfer to paper towels to drain and repeat with the remaining artichokes, adding more olive oil to the skillet as needed.

3. On a serving platter, swoop and swirl the Greek yogurt across the surface. Scatter the artichokes on top, then spoon the butter beans and herb oil evenly over the yogurt. Serve with a sprinkle of mint leaves, a pinch of pepper flakes, and lemon wedges for squeezing.

Warm Farro Salad *with* Dried Fruit

Serves 6 to 8

Words like "farro" and "lacinato kale" didn't really enter my vocabulary until I moved to San Francisco in my early 20s. Bay Area folks had a much larger culinary vocabulary than my family, who have their list of favorite ingredients and they're sticking to them, thank you very much. I learned "salad" could mean almost anything—and the lunch bars at Berkeley Bowl, Bi-Rite, and Rainbow Grocery were my greatest teachers. This hearty farro salad is a love story to California cooking with lots of fruity, citrusy flavors that pair perfectly with fish.

Make Ahead: The finished farro salad can be cooled, covered with cling wrap, and refrigerated up to 3 days.

2 cups farro, rinsed

4 cups vegetable broth

1 head lacinato kale, stems removed and leaves sliced into ribbons

Kosher salt and freshly ground black pepper

1 cup roasted almonds, roughly chopped

1 cup dried apricots, chopped

1 cup prunes, chopped

½ cup dried cranberries

½ cup dried currants

3 tablespoons extra-virgin olive oil

3 tablespoons Dijon mustard

2 tablespoons red wine vinegar

8 ounces feta cheese

1. In a large pot, stir together the farro and broth. Set over high heat to bring to a boil, then reduce the heat to medium. Cook, stirring occasionally, until the liquid is mostly absorbed and the farro is tender, 15 to 20 minutes.

2. Remove from the heat and add the kale along with a generous pinch each of salt and pepper. Stir in the kale to wilt, then add the almonds, apricots, prunes, cranberries, currants, olive oil, Dijon, and vinegar. Stir until everything is well combined. Crumble the feta over the top and fold in. Taste for seasoning and add more salt and pepper as needed.

3. Transfer the mixture to a large bowl and serve warm, or let cool completely, cover tightly with cling wrap, and refrigerate for at least 1 hour or up to 3 days to serve chilled.

Insalata di Frutti di Mare

Serves 8

Frutti di mare, or fruit of the sea, is a poetic way to describe this vibrant seafood salad. It is also a great way to describe me and my friends on one of our many trips to Fire Island, but that's a different kind of poem. The secret to this dish is in the gentle steaming, which keeps the mussels, shrimp, and calamari perfectly tender—none of that rubbery texture we sometimes associate with seafood. Pair that with crunchy fennel, sweet peppers, briny capers, and a zesty lemon dressing, and you've got a dish that's both refreshing and full of flavor. It's a seafood sonnet on a plate!

Make Ahead: The finished seafood salad can be refrigerated up to 24 hours.

I pound mussels, debearded and scrubbed

I pound large shrimp, peeled and deveined

I pound calamari, cleaned and cut into ½-inch rings, tentacles left whole

I large fennel bulb, thinly sliced, fronds reserved

12 mini sweet peppers, thinly sliced

½ cup fresh lemon juice (from 3 to 4 lemons)

½ cup extra-virgin olive oil

¼ cup roughly chopped fresh dill

¼ cup finely chopped fresh chives

3 tablespoons drained capers plus I tablespoon caper brine

Kosher salt and freshly ground black pepper

I. Set a stainless steel colander or steamer basket inside a large pot. Slowly pour in water to cover the bottom of the pot, stopping before it floods into the colander. Cover and set the whole contraption over medium-high heat. Bring the water to a boil, then reduce to medium-low for a steady simmer. Fill a medium bowl with ice water.

2. Arrange the mussels in the colander and cover. Cook for 8 to 10 minutes, checking periodically to transfer open mussels to paper towels to drain. When all the mussels are out (discard any that don't open after 10 minutes), arrange the shrimp in the colander, cover, and cook until bright pink and opaque, 3 to 4 minutes. Immediately transfer the shrimp to the ice water. Arrange the calamari in the colander, cover, and cook until opaque, 2 to 3 minutes more. Add to the ice water.

3. Meanwhile, in a large bowl, toss the fennel, fennel fronds, peppers, lemon juice, olive oil, dill, chives, capers, and caper brine and season with salt and black pepper. Drain the shrimp and calamari, pat dry, and add to the bowl along with the mussels. Toss everything together to coat well and taste for seasoning.

4. Cover tightly with cling wrap and refrigerate for at least I hour. Serve chilled.

Scallops *over* Angel Hair *with* Lemon & Tarragon

This pasta that is almost too pure for this world. Sweet, tender scallops are held in the arms of an angel hair while thin slices of lemon float away into a heavenly butter-wine sauce. Think of this recipe as a riff on classic linguine with clams, swapping out bulky shells for delicate scallops and adding lemon for a fresh twist. It's far from fussy yet still feels special, with all the precious flavors coming together gracefully and quickly.

Serves 6 to 8

I pound scallops

Kosher salt

I pound dried angel hair pasta

4 tablespoons extra-virgin olive oil

I lemon, quartered and thinly sliced

4 garlic cloves, thinly sliced

Freshly ground black pepper

I cup dry white wine

½ cup (I stick) unsalted butter

Juice of 2 lemons

½ cup roughly chopped fresh tarragon

I. Line a rimmed sheet pan with two layers of paper towels. Arrange the scallops on the towels, then gently press another layer on top. Set aside at room temperature to drain.

2. Bring a large pot of salted water to a boil over high heat. Add the pasta and cook to al dente according to package directions. Reserve ½ cup of the pasta cooking water, then drain.

3. Meanwhile, in a large nonstick skillet over medium heat, combine 2 tablespoons of the olive oil, the lemon, and the garlic. Season with salt and pepper and cook until the lemons are softened and the garlic begins to brown, about 5 minutes. Add the wine, butter, and a pinch of salt. Let the butter melt and the wine come to a simmer, about 2 minutes.

4. Add the pasta to the skillet along with the lemon juice and tarragon. Toss to combine, adding a splash of the reserved pasta cooking water as needed to help coat the pasta. Pile the pasta into a large serving bowl and cover with a clean kitchen towel to keep warm.

5. Wipe out the skillet and set it over high heat. Add the remaining 2 tablespoons olive oil and heat until just smoking. Uncover the scallops and season with salt and pepper. Arrange the scallops in an even layer, spacing them apart. Cook, undisturbed, until browned on the bottom, about 2 minutes, then flip and continue cooking until firm and cooked through, I to 2 minutes more.

6. Arrange the scallops on top of the pasta and serve immediately.

Roast Salmon *with* Smashed Olives

Serves 6 to 8

I love roasting salmon because it's such a forgiving fish, which is perfect for when I am entertaining slightly less forgiving guests (read: Italian Americans) during the holidays. Salting the fillet ahead of time not only seasons the flesh all the way through, but also helps it stay juicy even if you overcook it a little, plus it stops those white globs from leaking out. After it comes out of the oven, it rests in a mix of fresh orange juice, olive oil, and roughly chopped olives, so every bite is guaranteed to be moist and flavorful. I have always found that the best way to keep yapping mouths shut at the at the dinner table is to keep them full of food, and this salmon really does the trick.

6 tablespoons extra-virgin olive oil, plus more for greasing

I (4-pound) salmon fillet, or 2 (2-pound) salmon fillets

Kosher salt and freshly ground black pepper

Zest and juice of 2 large oranges

2 (10-ounce) jars pitted Castelvetrano olives, drained, smashed, and roughly chopped

½ cup finely chopped fresh parsley, plus more for garnish

1. Line a rimmed sheet pan with parchment paper and grease the surface with olive oil. Pat the salmon dry with paper towels and generously season the flesh with salt and pepper. Lay the salmon skin side down on the parchment and let marinate in the fridge for at least I hour or up to 8 hours.

2. Preheat the oven to 450°F. Drizzle 2 tablespoons of the olive oil over the salmon, then bake until golden brown on the edges and cooked through in the center (a thermometer inserted into the center should reach 125°F), 15 to 20 minutes.

3. Meanwhile, in a medium bowl, whisk together the remaining 4 tablespoons olive oil with the orange zest and juice and a big pinch each of salt and pepper. Fold in the olives and parsley.

4. When the salmon is done, spoon the dressing all over the surface. (Or transfer to a platter before spooning the dressing.) Let the rest for 5 minutes before serving.

Joyuary

Make THE Menu

● 1 DAY BEFORE

Two Kinds of Roasted Tomatoes with Burrata & Prosciutto: Make the tomatoes and store in the fridge.

Garlicky Cauliflower Mash: Make the mash and store in the fridge.

Charred Broccoli with Anchovy Vinaigrette: Blanch the broccoli and store in the fridge.

Chicken Cordon Bimpy: Assemble the chicken and store in the fridge.

Key Lime Pie Bars: Make the base and filling, without topping. Store in the fridge.

● 2 HOURS BEFORE

Key Lime Pie Bars: Trim the edges, top with meringue, and store in the fridge.

JANUARY GETS A BAD RAP, BUT I WANT TO CHANGE THAT narrative. I know January *can* be tough for a lot of people, whether because of the cold weather, early sunsets, post-holiday blues, or pressure (societal or self) to set unachievable goals or start a strict diet. I have been there too many times myself, and now, January is a—no, *the*—month of joy, not dread. After the whirlwind of the holidays, it's my time to relax at home with my family, my friends, and Gus. The hustle and bustle has died down, and we can finally embrace the bliss of doing nothing.

For me, this time is about the sweet simplicity of being together. I recap the past year, get excited for the one ahead, and find comfort in doing what I love. Planning delicious get-togethers and happy gatherings can turn a gloomy January into a month of self-love, happiness, and freedom from unnecessary expectations for myself and for others. Embrace where you are (hopefully on the couch with a lovely snack) and find the Joyuary in the little things. This year and every year, my only resolution is to keep eating what I love and letting food bring joy to those around me!

● **1 HOUR BEFORE**

Two Kinds of Roasted Tomatoes with Burrata & Prosciutto: Remove the tomatoes from the fridge to come to room temperature.

Chicken Cordon Bimpy: Remove the chicken from the fridge to come to room temperature.

● **30 MINUTES BEFORE**

Garlicky Cauliflower Mash: Reheat the mash.

Charred Broccoli with Anchovy Vinaigrette: Make the dressing, cook the broccoli, and assemble. Cover with foil to keep warm.

● **15 MINUTES BEFORE**

Fettuccine Alfredo: Make the sauce and pasta.

● **10 MINUTES BEFORE**

Chicken Cordon Bimpy: Bake the chicken.

● **SERVING TIME**

Two Kinds of Roasted Tomatoes with Burrata & Prosciutto: Assemble the burrata.

Key Lime Pie Bars: Torch the meringue and cut into bars for dessert.

Two Kinds of Roasted Tomatoes *with* Burrata & Prosciutto

Serves 6 to 8

Listen, if we are doing things that make us happy without judgment, I am going to create a recipe that is mostly tomatoes. Deal with it! Roasting sweet cherry tomatoes and tangy sun-dried tomatoes (they have been through a lot already, but trust me here) together creates an incredible mix of texture and flavor. Then, creamy hunks of burrata are surrounded by an herby, vinegary oil and rich slices of salty prosciutto. No one needs to know how easy this was to make (though you can feel free to direct them to this page), but they *do* need to know how delicious it is to eat (again, feel free to direct them to this page). And for our vegetarian friends, just skip the prosciutto or serve it on the side—they deserve to be happy without judgment, too!

Make Ahead The tomato mixture can be refrigerated in an airtight container up to 3 days; bring to room temperature before serving.

1 pint cherry tomatoes, halved

1 (7-ounce) jar julienne-cut sun-dried tomatoes in oil

1 garlic clove, grated

Kosher salt and freshly ground black pepper

2 tablespoons red wine vinegar

1 teaspoon dried oregano

½ teaspoon red pepper flakes

6 ounces thinly sliced prosciutto

2 (8-ounce) fresh burrata balls

Flaky salt

1. Preheat the oven to 450°F.

2. In an 8-inch square baking dish, toss the cherry tomatoes with the sun-dried tomatoes and their oil. Stir in the garlic and a good pinch each of salt and black pepper. Bake for about 15 minutes, stirring halfway, until the cherry tomatoes are soft and just beginning to char in some spots.

3. Remove from the oven, stir in the vinegar, oregano, and pepper flakes and let cool for at least 30 minutes.

4. Arrange the prosciutto around a platter. In the center of the plate, pierce the burrata to break them open, then spoon the tomato mixture on top. Finish with a sprinkle of flaky salt and a few cracks of pepper before serving.

Garlicky Cauliflower Mash

Serves 6 to 8

Alright, I'm about to make a bold claim: potatoes have finally met their mash. This cauliflower mash is just as good as, if not better than, mashed potatoes. I said what I said—and I meant it! Not only is cutie cauli easier to whip up, but it's also just as creamy. My version is packed with rich flavor from olive oil and toasted garlic. Equally perfect for a Wednesday night or a holiday, I make this all the time and still can't get enough. Start mashing—once you try it, you'll want to call me raving! I will pick up, I promise.

Make Ahead The cauliflower mash can be refrigerated in an airtight container up to 3 days.

Kosher salt

2 large heads cauliflower, cut into florets

½ cup extra-virgin olive oil, plus more for serving

8 garlic cloves, smashed

Freshly ground black pepper

Red pepper flakes

1. Bring a large pot of salted water to a boil over high heat. Add the cauliflower and cook until very tender, about 15 minutes. Reserve 1 cup of the cooking water, then drain the cauliflower and return it to the pot.

2. Meanwhile, in a small skillet or saucepan, combine the olive oil, garlic, a few grinds of black pepper, and pepper flakes. Cook over medium heat until the garlic is golden brown and a little bit crispy on the edges, about 10 minutes. Remove from the heat and set aside to infuse.

3. Add the infused oil and garlic to the pot with the drained cauliflower. Use a potato masher or immersion blender to blend the cauliflower and garlic into a chunky mash. If it's too thick, add splashes of the reserved cooking water until the consistency is perfect. Taste for seasoning and add more salt as needed.

4. Scoop the mash into a serving bowl and use a spoon to swirl some peaks and valleys on top. Drizzle olive oil around to make beautiful pools, then finish with red pepper flakes before serving.

Charred Broccoli *with* Anchovy Vinaigrette

Serves 6 to 8

Cooking is all about giving way to whatever tickles your taste buds. For me, that's charring food to extreme crispiness, embracing the briny flavor of anchovies, and eating giant chunks of cheese. This dish collects all that happiness together in one place. I like to peel the tough outer layer from the broccoli, so I can cut extra-long florets that reach about halfway down the stem, then use the tip of a paring knife to crumble the Parmesan in large chunks, giving nice, bulky bites to the dish. Charring the broccoli florets gives them an almost smoky flavor, while the anchovy vinaigrette brings a bold kick. And if you've only ever had grated parm, these big shards are about to blow your cheese-loving mind.

Make Ahead The broccoli can be boiled and refrigerated in an airtight container up to 24 hours; bring to room temperature before cooking.

Kosher salt

2 large heads broccoli, stems peeled, cut into large florets

Zest and juice of 1 lemon, plus 2 more lemons, halved

2 tablespoons white wine vinegar

1 (2-ounce) tin anchovies in oil

1 garlic clove

Freshly ground black pepper

¾ cup extra-virgin olive oil

2 ounces Parmesan cheese, cut into large hunks

1. Bring a large pot of salted water to a boil over high heat. Add the broccoli and cook until bright green and barely tender, about 5 minutes. Drain well.

2. In a blender, combine the lemon zest and lemon juice with the vinegar, anchovies and their oil, garlic, and a pinch each of salt and pepper. Blend on low speed to combine, about 30 seconds. Add ½ cup of the olive oil and blend again until smooth. Taste for seasoning and add more salt as needed.

3. In a large nonstick skillet, heat the remaining ¼ cup olive oil over high heat until just smoking. Add the broccoli and cook until charred on the bottom, about 6 minutes, then transfer to a serving bowl. Place the lemon halves cut side down in the oil and cook until charred, about 3 minutes. Transfer to the serving bowl.

4. Toss the Parmesan hunks and broccoli together and arrange the lemons on the side. Spoon the dressing over the broccoli, reserving some to serve on the side, if you like. Finish the broccoli with pepper and a squeeze of the charred lemon before serving.

Fettuccine Alfredo

Serves 6 to 8

My lifelong love affair with fettuccine Alfredo is thanks to my parents, who let me order it at almost every meal without judgment for a solid four to twelve years of my childhood. It was the first of many affirmations that we can eat whatever makes us happy. This recipe is a creamy, comforting classic that never fails to bring back the spirit of baby Grossy. Food should be about pure, unadulterated joy, and fettuccine Alfredo is a crowd-pleaser, just be sure to eat it with a smile on your face.

Kosher salt

1 pound dried fettuccine pasta

4 tablespoons (½ stick) unsalted butter

1 shallot, diced

1 garlic clove, minced

Freshly ground black pepper

2 cups heavy cream

1 cup freshly grated Parmesan cheese, plus more for serving

½ cup finely chopped fresh parsley

1. Bring a large pot of salted water to a boil over high heat. Add the fettuccine and cook for 2 minutes less than al dente according to package directions. Reserve 1 cup of the pasta cooking water, then drain.

2. Melt the butter in a large skillet over medium heat. Add the shallot, garlic, and a pinch each of salt and pepper. Cook, stirring occasionally, until the shallot is soft and translucent, about 3 minutes. Stir in the heavy cream and cook until reduced slightly, about 2 minutes.

3. Add the fettucine to the sauce over medium heat. Toss to coat, then add the Parmesan and ¼ cup of the reserved pasta cooking water. Continue to toss as the cheese melts and the sauce thickens. Add another ¼ cup of pasta water and continue to toss until a thick and glossy sauce coats the pasta. (Add more water as needed or stop here.)

4. Remove from the heat and taste for seasoning and add more salt and pepper as needed. Sprinkle on the parsley, more Parmesan, and more pepper before serving.

Chicken Cordon Bimpy

Serves 8

This recipe is a certified Bimpy classic. An easy Italian twist on the traditional chicken cordon bleu, you won't be surprised to know it starts with a gently pan-fried chicken cutlet instead of a fussy stuffed chicken breast. From there, a mix of deli ham, sliced provolone, and jarred roasted red peppers (all things you can grab at any store) pile onto the cutlets, and everything bakes until the cheese is perfectly melted. Simple to make, a joy to devour, and even better to enjoy as leftovers, this dish has saved me countless times for last-minute dinners and parties.

Make Ahead *The chicken can be assembled, covered with cling wrap, and refrigerated up to 24 hours; bring to room temperature before baking.*

4 boneless, skinless chicken breasts

1 cup all-purpose flour

2 teaspoons kosher salt

1 teaspoon freshly ground black pepper

1 teaspoon garlic powder

1 teaspoon onion powder

1 teaspoon dried oregano

10 tablespoons extra-virgin olive oil

1 pound thick-sliced deli ham, cut into ½-inch pieces

1 large white onion, diced

1 (16-ounce) jar roasted red peppers, drained

8 slices provolone cheese

1. Preheat the oven to 400°F.

2. Working one at a time, slice each chicken breast horizontally to butterfly, then cut down the middle to make two pieces. Bang with a meat mallet or rolling pin to evenly flatten each piece to about ½ inch thick. On a large plate, whisk together the flour, salt, pepper, garlic powder, onion powder, and oregano. Lightly dredge the chicken in the flour, turning to coat and shaking off any excess.

3. Heat 2 tablespoons of the olive oil in a large nonstick skillet over medium-high heat. When the oil is shimmering, arrange two of the coated breasts in the skillet. Cook until golden brown on the outside and cooked through inside, 4 to 6 minutes per side, then transfer to a rimmed sheet pan. Add another 2 tablespoons olive oil to the skillet and repeat with the remaining chicken.

4. Add the remaining 2 tablespoons olive oil to the same skillet over medium heat. Add the ham and onion to the skillet and cook, stirring often, until the onion is softened, about 5 minutes. Scoop the mixture onto the chicken, dividing evenly. Lay a roasted pepper on top of each and finish with a slice of provolone.

5. Bake until the cheese is melted and golden brown, 8 to 10 minutes. Serve the chicken directly from the sheet pan or transfer to a serving platter.

Key Lime Pie Bars

Makes 9 or 12 bars

One year during college on a spring break trip to Key West, I fell in love, hard and fast, with key lime pie. I think I ate it approximately thirty-seven times in five days. A few years later, I dated a guy mainly to get close to his aunt, whom I fell in love with, hard and fast (the aunt, not the guy), because she would fly to San Francisco with Steve's Key Lime Pie from Brooklyn just for me. This recipe turns one of the loves of life (the pie, not the aunt) into an easy bar form for streamlined baking, slicing, and serving . . . and eating. Layers of extra-thick graham cracker crust, tart lime filling, and sweet clouds of meringue make these bars impossible not to fall in love with.

Make Ahead The filled bars can be covered with cling wrap and refrigerated up to 24 hours. The meringue can be made up to 4 hours before serving.

Nonstick cooking spray

CRUST

2 sleeves graham crackers (18 sheets)

½ cup sugar

½ cup (1 stick) unsalted butter, melted

2 large egg whites

FILLING

6 large egg yolks

2 tablespoons cornstarch

2 (14-ounce) cans sweetened condensed milk

1 cup Key lime juice or fresh lime juice (from 4 to 5 limes)

½ teaspoon kosher salt

MERINGUE

4 large egg whites, at room temperature

½ teaspoon cream of tartar

⅓ cup sugar

1. Preheat the oven to 350°F. Line an 8-inch square baking dish with parchment paper, leaving a 1-inch overhang on each side, then coat with nonstick spray.

2. **MAKE THE CRUST:** In a food processor, pulse the graham crackers until broken down into fine crumbs. Add the sugar, butter, and egg whites and process until combined. Transfer the mixture to the prepared pan and press it into an even layer along the bottom. Bake for about 20 minutes, until lightly golden brown.

3. **MEANWHILE, MAKE THE FILLING:** In a medium bowl, whisk together the egg yolks and cornstarch. Add the condensed milk, lime juice, and salt and whisk again until well combined.

4. When the crust is ready, remove it from the oven and pour in the filling. Lightly tap the pan against the counter to burst any air bubbles. Bake for 8 to 10 minutes, until the filling is set on the surface but still has some give when you wiggle the baking dish. Let cool completely, then cover with cling wrap and refrigerate for at least 4 hours or up to 24 hours.

5. **MAKE THE MERINGUE:** In a stand mixer fitted with the whisk attachment, beat the egg whites on medium speed until light and frothy, about 1 minute. Add the cream of tartar and beat until soft peaks form. With the mixer running, slowly add the sugar, about 1 tablespoon at a time, until stiff, glossy peaks form.

6. Remove the pan from the fridge and use the parchment overhang to lift the bars out and place on a cutting board. Trim the edges so all four sides are even. Scoop and swirl the meringue over the top. Then, only if you're feeling fancy, use a kitchen blowtorch to lightly brown the surface of the meringue.

7. Cut into 9 or 12 bars, depending on how large you want them. Transfer to a platter and refrigerate until ready to serve, up to 4 hours.

Girls' Night In

Make THE Menu

● **3 DAYS BEFORE**

Celery Mocktini: Make the celery shrub and store in the fridge.

● **2 DAYS BEFORE**

Roasted Shrimp Cocktail: Make the cocktail sauce and roast the shrimp. Store separately in the fridge.

A Shareable Wedge Salad: Make the dressing, onions, bacon, and breadcrumbs. Store all separately in the fridge.

● **1 DAY BEFORE**

Clams Casino: Assemble the clams and store in the fridge.

Chocolate Cream Pie for Bimpy: Make the pie without topping and store in the fridge.

FROM VALENTINE'S TO GALENTINE'S AND EVERY TYPE
of date night in between, nothing says romance, at least not to me, like a
nice, big, juicy piece of red meat. Getting all dolled up for a night out at
your favorite steakhouse is great, but cooking a classic steakhouse meal
for your lover or your friends at home? Possibly in your pajamas? That's
real luxury. This menu allows you to do just that—whether it's pure
romance or just us girls.

You have my permission invite the gals over, tell everyone to tie up
their hair in a messy bun, put on their stretchy pants, and get ready for
a cozy night in. Whether you're celebrating a promotion, a birthday, an
anniversary, or just the joy of being together, the magic is in the details,
and this chapter has everything you need to make a medium-rare
evening with the girlies well-done.

● **1 HOUR BEFORE**

Steak over Frites: Make the
fries and steaks. Cover with
foil to keep warm.

● **15 MINUTES BEFORE**

Creamy Dreamy Spinach:
Make the creamed spinach.

A Shareable Wedge Salad:
Assemble the salad.

● **5 MINUTES BEFORE**

Roasted Shrimp Cocktail:
Arrange the shrimp and
sauce.

Clams Casino: Bake the
clams.

● **SERVING TIME**

Steak over Frites: Slice the
steak and arrange on a
platter.

Celery Mocktini: Mix and
serve the drink.

**Chocolate Cream Pie for
Bimpy:** Top and serve for
dessert.

Roasted Shrimp Cocktail

Serves 6 to 8

My eyes always light up when I see this hors d'oeuvres legend at a party (or at a Costco), but when I'm entertaining at home, I consider *roasted* shrimp cocktail to be one of my greatest party tricks. I skip the drama of blanching by simply tossing the shrimp with lemon, salt, and pepper and roasting them in the oven to lock in that flavor. My easy-peasy homemade cocktail sauce is heavy on the horseradish and lemon for just the right amount of tangy heat. Whether I'm hosting a party or just making dinner for Gus and me, this roasted shrimp cocktail is the way to go.

Make Ahead The cocktail sauce can be refrigerated in an airtight container up to 3 days. The cooked, cooled shrimp can be refrigerated in an airtight container up to 3 days.

COCKTAIL SAUCE

I cup ketchup

¼ cup prepared horseradish

Zest and juice of I lemon

I tablespoon Worcestershire sauce

I teaspoon freshly ground black pepper

I teaspoon hot sauce

Kosher salt

SHRIMP

Zest and juice of I lemon, plus 2 lemons, cut into wedges

2 tablespoons dry white wine

I tablespoon extra-virgin olive oil

2 teaspoons freshly ground black pepper

I teaspoon kosher salt

2 pounds jumbo tail-on shrimp, peeled and deveined

1. Preheat the oven to 450°F.

2. **MAKE THE COCKTAIL SAUCE:** In a medium bowl, whisk the ketchup, horseradish, lemon zest, lemon juice, Worcestershire, pepper, hot sauce, and a pinch of salt. Taste for seasoning and add more salt as needed, then cover tightly with cling wrap and refrigerate until ready to use.

3. **MAKE THE SHRIMP:** In a large bowl, whisk together the lemon zest, lemon juice, wine, olive oil, pepper, and salt. Add the shrimp and toss to coat. Arrange the shrimp on a rimmed sheet pan in a single layer and pour any remaining marinade over the top.

4. Roast the shrimp for 8 to 10 minutes, until bright pink and opaque. Immediately transfer to a plate and refrigerate for at least I hour.

5. Arrange the cold shrimp and cocktail sauce on a platter and serve with the lemon wedges.

Clams Casino

Serves 6 to 8

Two restaurants live inside of me: One is a classic New England seafood joint, and the other is an old-school Italian American trattoria. The one item on both menus is clams casino, a fancier version of baked clams that was born in Rhode Island and adopted by Italian Americans. This extremely extra (obviously?) version is packed with bacon, Parmesan, fresh parsley, chives, garlic, and butter—and that's just the topping! No matter what restaurant lives inside of you, this showstopper is a foolproof way to turn any meal into a five-star event.

Make Ahead *The assembled clams can be tightly wrapped in cling wrap and refrigerated up to 24 hours.*

BUTTER

½ cup (1 stick) unsalted butter, at room temperature

1 shallot, diced

1 garlic clove, diced

2 tablespoons finely chopped fresh parsley

2 tablespoons finely chopped fresh chives

½ teaspoon kosher salt

¼ teaspoon red pepper flakes

BREADCRUMBS

4 slices bacon, finely diced

⅔ cup panko breadcrumbs

¼ cup finely chopped fresh parsley

Kosher salt

CLAMS

½ cup dry white wine

24 littleneck clams, scrubbed

Kosher salt

2 lemons, cut into wedges

1. **MAKE THE BUTTER:** In a small bowl, mash together the butter, shallots, garlic, parsley, chives, salt, and pepper flakes.

2. **MAKE THE BREADCRUMBS:** Arrange the bacon in a single layer in a large skillet. Cook over medium heat, stirring occasionally, until the fat is rendered and the bacon is crisp, about 8 minutes. Add the panko and stir until golden brown, about 3 minutes. Remove from the heat and stir in the parsley and a good pinch of salt. Transfer to a small bowl.

3. **MAKE THE CLAMS:** Preheat the oven to 450°F.

4. Return the pan from the breadcrumbs to medium heat (no need to wipe it out). Add the wine and bring to a simmer. Add the clams in an even layer, then cover and cook, checking every few minutes to transfer the opened clams to a large bowl, until all the clams have opened, 8 to 10 minutes. Discard any clams that do not open after 10 minutes. Let the clams cool slightly.

5. Fill a rimmed sheet pan with a layer of kosher salt, just deep enough to hold the clams. Working with one at a time, pry the top shells off the clams. Spread 1 teaspoon of butter over each clam, then sprinkle the panko onto the butter. Nestle the clams into the salt.

6. Bake the clams for 5 minutes, until the butter is melted and the breadcrumbs are warmed through. Serve immediately, directly from the sheet pan with plenty of lemon wedges alongside for squeezing.

Creamy Dreamy Spinach

Serves 6 to 8

Creamed spinach is a staple at any steakhouse for a reason: It's incredible. My version starts with fresh, whole spinach leaves (instead of frozen and chopped) that wilt perfectly as they melt into a buttery onion and garlic base and get wrapped up in a creamy, cheesy sauce. The combination of tangy cream cheese and nutty Parmesan adds a luxurious flavor that pairs beautifully with everything from steak (duh) to salmon to roasted chicken.

3 tablespoons unsalted butter

1 medium yellow onion, diced

4 garlic cloves, thinly sliced

Kosher salt and freshly ground black pepper

2 (8-ounce) bags fresh baby spinach

4 ounces cream cheese, cubed

¼ cup freshly grated Parmesan cheese

Ground nutmeg

1. In a large skillet or saucepan, melt the butter over medium heat. Add the onion, garlic, and a big pinch each of salt and pepper. Cook, stirring occasionally, until the onion is softened, about 5 minutes.

2. Working in batches, add the spinach, stirring to wilt and make room for more. Add the cream cheese and stir until melted and incorporated, about 2 minutes. Cook, stirring occasionally, until the sauce is thickened, about 8 minutes.

3. Remove from the heat and stir in the Parmesan. Taste for seasoning and add more salt and pepper as needed. Finish with nutmeg to taste before serving.

A Shareable Wedge Salad

Serves 6 to 8

I'm a fan of iceberg lettuce, and I won't apologize for it. It's cold, crisp, and the perfect sturdy base for lots of toppings and dressing. When I have an entire wedge salad all to myself, I will gleefully attack the whole thing with my knife and fork like Michelangelo sculpting David. But when I'm sharing it with friends, things can get a little dicey with all that silverware flying. The solution is mini wedges, giving each person their share of all the toppings: pickled red onions, crumbles of bacon, crispy panko (toasted in the bacon fat!), sweet cherry tomatoes, and, most important, a very thick-and-chunky blue cheese dressing.

Make Ahead *The dressing, onions, bacon, and breadcrumbs can be refrigerated in separate airtight containers up to 3 days.*

BLUE CHEESE DRESSING

3 tablespoons sour cream

3 tablespoons mayonnaise

2 tablespoons buttermilk

2 tablespoons white wine vinegar

½ teaspoon sugar

½ teaspoon garlic powder

½ teaspoon freshly ground black pepper

¼ teaspoon kosher salt

½ cup (3 ounces) crumbled blue cheese, plus more for serving

SALAD

½ medium red onion, thinly sliced

½ cup red wine vinegar

Kosher salt

4 slices thick-cut bacon

½ cup panko breadcrumbs

1 head iceberg lettuce

½ cup cherry tomatoes, quartered

2 tablespoons finely chopped fresh chives

1. MAKE THE DRESSING: In a medium bowl, whisk the sour cream, mayonnaise, buttermilk, vinegar, sugar, garlic powder, pepper, and salt. Stir in the blue cheese. Cover tightly with cling wrap and refrigerate until ready to use.

2. MAKE THE SALAD: In a small, shallow bowl, toss the onion rings and vinegar with a pinch of salt. Set aside to marinate.

3. Lay the bacon slices in a single layer in a large skillet. Cook over medium heat, flipping halfway, until the bacon is crisp, 8 to 10 minutes. Transfer to paper towels to drain. Sprinkle the panko into the skillet and cook, stirring constantly, until the panko is golden brown, 1 to 2 minutes. Transfer to paper towels to drain.

4. To assemble the salad, cut the iceberg head into quarters, then cut the quarters in half to make 8 pyramids. Arrange the mini wedges on a serving platter and spoon the dressing over the tops. Drain the onions and arrange them over the salad, followed by the tomatoes and an extra sprinkle of blue cheese. Crumble the bacon all over and finish with the panko and chives before serving.

Steak
over Frites

Serves 6 to 8

Patiently watching herby compound butter melt over a perfectly seasoned, perfectly cooked steak is the pinnacle of the steakhouse experience. In this recipe, the steak is cooked in the oven to medium (or shorter or longer—you decide) then quickly seared *after,* so you can prepare multiple steaks and still serve them with a perfectly browned outside and warm inside. The fries are double-fried so they're extra crisp and tossed with a mix of parsley and Parmesan so there's flavor everywhere you turn. Perfection on a plate!

3 (1-pound) rib eye steaks, about 1 inch thick

Kosher salt and freshly ground black pepper

½ cup (1 stick) unsalted butter, at room temperature

2 garlic cloves, chopped

2 tablespoons finely chopped fresh herbs, such as parsley, rosemary, thyme, or sage

1 tablespoon finely chopped fresh chives

2 quarts plus 2 tablespoons neutral oil

4 russet potatoes, peeled and cut into ¼-inch-wide fries, soaked in water for 10 minutes, and drained

¼ cup freshly grated Parmesan cheese

2 tablespoons chopped fresh parsley

1. Preheat the oven to 250°F. Set a wire rack over a rimmed sheet pan.

2. Pat the steaks dry with paper towels and generously season all over with salt and pepper. Set on the wire rack. In a small bowl, mash together the butter, garlic, herbs, chives, ½ teaspoon salt, and ½ teaspoon pepper.

3. Meanwhile, fit a large Dutch oven with a thermometer, then add 2 quarts of the oil. Heat over medium heat to 325°F.

4. Add half the fries to the oil and cook until soft but not yet taking on color, about 5 minutes. Transfer to paper towels to drain. Allow the oil to return to 325°F and repeat with the remaining fries.

5. Transfer the steaks to the oven and bake for about 10 minutes, until a thermometer inserted in the thickest part registers 105°F (see Note). Halfway through cooking, set a large cast-iron skillet over high heat.

6. Meanwhile, increase the heat under the Dutch oven so the oil temperature reaches 375°F. Working in two batches again, return the fries to the oil and cook until lightly golden brown, about 3 minutes per batch. Transfer to

fresh paper towels to drain and sprinkle generously with salt.

7. Add the remaining 2 tablespoons oil to the hot skillet and swirl to coat. Immediately add the steaks, working in batches as needed. Cook until a golden brown crust forms and a thermometer inserted into the thickest part registers 135°F (see Note), about 2 minutes per side. Transfer to a cutting board and spread the butter mixture over the top, dividing it evenly among the steaks.

8. In a large bowl, working in batches as needed, toss the fries with the Parmesan and parsley to coat. Spread out on a serving platter. Slice the steaks against the grain and arrange on top of the fries, drizzling any collected butter and juices over top. Serve immediately.

Note

For medium-rare, bake for about 6 minutes, until an instant-read thermometer inserted into the thickest part registers 95°F, then sear until it registers 125°F. For well-done, bake for about 20 minutes, until an instant-read thermometer inserted into the thickest part registers 125°F, then sear until it registers 160°F.

Chocolate Cream Pie *for* Bimpy

Serves 6 to 8

If Girls' Night were to have a mascot, it would be my 103-year-old grandfather, Bimpy. There is nothing he loves more than telling jokes and sharing a century's worth of gossip—except possibly eating chocolate cream pie. Quite literally every family gathering for my entire life has featured a chocolate cream pie for Bimpy. It's made with My-T-Fine chocolate pudding poured into a store-bought crust and topped with Reddi-Wip, and it brings him great happiness. After many years of whipping up that precious recipe, I've created a version for him from my heart and from scratch. Ladies, trust me, he deserves it, and so do we! Just don't forget to save him a slice . . . or two!

Make Ahead The pie dough can be wrapped and refrigerated up to 2 days. The filled pie, without topping, can be covered and refrigerated up to 24 hours.

CRUST

1½ cups all-purpose flour, plus more for dusting

2 teaspoons granulated sugar

½ teaspoon kosher salt

½ cup (I stick) unsalted butter, cubed and chilled

2 to 3 tablespoons ice water

FILLING

½ cup granulated sugar

¼ cup cornstarch

3 tablespoons unsweetened cocoa powder

½ teaspoon kosher salt

3 cups whole milk

6 ounces bittersweet chocolate, chopped

4 tablespoons (½ stick) unsalted butter, cubed

I teaspoon pure vanilla extract

Nonstick cooking spray

TOPPING

I cup heavy cream

3 tablespoons powdered sugar

Chocolate shavings or unsweetened cocoa powder

I. MAKE THE CRUST: In a food processor, combine the flour, granulated sugar, and salt. Pulse two times just to mix. Add the butter and process until a rough dough forms, about 30 seconds. Add 2 tablespoons of ice water and process until the dough pulls together. Add up to I more tablespoon ice water as needed. Press the dough into a disc and wrap tightly with cling wrap. Refrigerate for at least 2 hours or up to 2 days.

2. Lightly dust a work surface with flour. Roll out the pie crust, adding more flour as needed, into a 12-inch circle. Transfer the crust to a 9-inch pie plate and crimp the edges. Cover the dough with parchment paper and fill with pie weights or dried beans. Chill in the fridge for about 30 minutes.

3. Preheat the oven to 400°F.

4. Bake the pie crust until the bottom and edges are golden brown, 30 to 35 minutes. Let the crust cool completely, then remove the weights and parchment.

5. MEANWHILE, MAKE THE FILLING: In a large saucepan, whisk the granulated sugar, cornstarch, cocoa powder, and salt. Slowly add the milk, whisking constantly to avoid clumps, until combined. Run a spatula around the sides and bottom to be sure everything is incorporated.

6. Set the saucepan over medium heat. Cook, whisking constantly, until the mixture is bubbling and reaches a thick pudding consistency, IO to I2 minutes, then remove from the heat. Immediately add the chopped chocolate and butter and whisk until fully melted. Whisk in the vanilla.

7. Scrape the filling into the pie crust, smoothing out the top (see Note, page 200). Coat a piece of parchment with nonstick spray and press it directly onto the top of the filling. Refrigerate for at least 4 hours to set, or up to 24 hours.

RECIPE CONTINUES

8. MAKE THE TOPPING: In a large bowl, combine the cream and powdered sugar. Using a handheld mixer on medium, whip until stiff peaks form, about 3 minutes. Discard the parchment from the top of the pie. Spread the whipped cream over the top, then finish with chocolate shavings and/or a dusting of cocoa powder. Serve immediately.

Note

Depending on the depth of your pie dish, you might have some filling left over. Luckily, it's a perfect chocolate pudding all on its own!

Celery Mocktini

Makes 6 drinks

When I think of a Girls' Night (out or in), I think of the most iconic girls first: Carrie, Charlotte, Miranda, and Samantha. Everyone says the city was the fifth character, but I would argue it was the cocktail glass. And I get it: When I'm with my girls, I, too, want something iconic and elegant to sip on while we talk about boys. In place of a boozy Cosmopolitan, I like this sweet, tart celery shrub. Making a shrub is as simple as combining sugar, vinegar, and (usually) fruit, but in this case celery, with herbs and spices. After it mingles and mellows for a couple days, the shrub is the perfect base for refreshing drinks and cocktails. If you do want to add booze, a splash of gin or vodka would fit right in.

Make Ahead The celery shrub can be refrigerated in an airtight container up to 3 days.

2 pounds celery, chopped

1 teaspoon whole black peppercorns

½ teaspoon kosher salt

¾ cup white wine vinegar

½ cup sugar

Extra-virgin olive oil, for serving

1. In a blender or food processor, combine the celery, peppercorns, salt, and ½ cup cold water. Process on high for 1 minute until the celery is pureed.

2. Set two layers of cheesecloth or a thin, clean kitchen towel in a colander and place the colander over a tall bowl. Pour the celery puree through the cheesecloth and let it drain. Gather the edges of the cheesecloth and squeeze to release any remaining liquid. You should have about 4 cups of celery water.

3. In a large airtight container, stir together the celery water, vinegar, and sugar. Cover tightly and refrigerate overnight or up to 3 days to allow the flavors to meld, shaking a couple times to make sure the sugar is fully dissolved.

4. Just before serving, stir the shrub (don't shake!) to reincorporate any separation. Divide the shrub among coupe glasses or martini glasses. Dot the surface with olive oil and serve.

Go for the *Gold*

Make THE Menu

● 2 DAYS BEFORE

Pineapple Fennel Pulled Pork Sliders: Make the pulled pork and store in the fridge.

● 1 DAY BEFORE

Coconut Shrimp with Spicy Peach Dip: Coat the shrimp and make the sauce. Store separately in the fridge.

Puttin' on the Ritz Crab Dip: Make the crab mixture and store in the fridge.

Nachos Grossy: Make the pico and steak. Store separately in the fridge.

Caramelized Banana Pudding: Assemble the pudding and store in the fridge.

THE OSCARS ARE MY SUPER BOWL, AND I WAIT

through all of awards season for this grand finale. Other must-watches throughout the year include the Grammys, Emmys, and Tonys. Gus loves sports (how did I get so lucky?!) and wants to watch every playoff and final, including the *actual* Super Bowl and the Olympics. All things considered, we find ourselves rooting for (screaming at) various things on television from the couch pretty often. What I've learned is whichever we're watching, the menus are interchangeable.

Of course, any big TV event is always better when you invite friends over to watch with you. And when I'm quietly sobbing at a Best Supporting Actress speech, I know I better have plenty of food at the ready to keep everyone satisfied . . . and quiet. Awards shows and Super Bowls are hours-long affairs, so, naturally, a big spread of perfect apps is exactly what I want to eat while I watch them. It's not the time to get fancy (save that for the red carpet); rather, this is an evening of paper plates, easy bites, and being crammed into the living room together. Okay, now everyone be quiet, I'm about to announce the nominees for Best Appetizer . . .

● **90 MINUTES BEFORE**

Gold Rush Wings: Bake the wings and toss with the sauce. Cover with foil to keep warm.

● **30 MINUTES BEFORE**

Puttin' on the Ritz Crab Dip: Bake the dip.

Pineapple Fennel Pulled Pork Sliders: Reheat the pulled pork.

● **15 MINUTES BEFORE**

Nachos Grossy: Assemble and bake the nachos.

Coconut Shrimp with Spicy Peach Dip: Cook the shrimp and set out the sauce.

● **5 MINUTES BEFORE**

Pineapple Fennel Pulled Pork Sliders: Assemble the sliders.

● **SERVING TIME**

Puttin' on the Ritz Crab Dip: Garnish the dip and serve with baguette slices.

Caramelized Banana Pudding: Serve for dessert.

Coconut Shrimp *with* Spicy Peach Dip

Serves 6 to 8

One of my favorite places to visit is the rainforest. Lush vegetation, animal life, rainstorms, a gift shop, and, most important, crispy coconut shrimp. Oh! Sorry, I meant the Rainforest Cafe! When an expedition to the mall is out of reach, I luckily can pull this easy recipe out of my safari hat. Imagine crispy, crunchy battered shrimp, with flecks of coconut and lime zest, dipped into a sauce of peach jam with lime and sriracha. The combination of textures and flavors makes for an unforgettable trip.

Make Ahead The dip can be refrigerated in an airtight container up to 3 days. The coated shrimp can be covered with cling wrap and refrigerated up to 24 hours.

DIP

½ cup peach or apricot jam

2 teaspoons fresh lime juice

1 teaspoon sriracha or hot sauce of your choice

SHRIMP

1 ¾ cups all-purpose flour

1 (13.5-ounce) can coconut milk

2 large eggs

2 teaspoons kosher salt

2½ cups unsweetened coconut flakes

½ cup panko breadcrumbs

Zest of 2 limes

1½ pounds jumbo shrimp, peeled, tails left on, and deveined

2 quarts neutral oil

1. **MAKE THE DIP:** In a small bowl, whisk the jam, lime juice, and hot sauce. Cover tightly with cling wrap and refrigerate until ready to use.

2. **MAKE THE SHRIMP:** In a shallow bowl, spread out ¾ cup of the flour. In a second shallow bowl, whisk the remaining 1 cup flour with the coconut milk, eggs, and salt. In a third shallow bowl, stir together the coconut flakes, panko, and lime zest. Line a rimmed sheet pan with parchment paper.

3. Pat the shrimp dry with paper towels. Working with one at a time, toss the shrimp to coat in the flour. Dip into the eggy batter, letting any excess drip off, then drop into the coconut-flake coating, pressing to adhere. Arrange the battered shrimp on the prepared sheet pan. Repeat with the remaining shrimp, then transfer the sheet pan to the fridge, uncovered, for 30 minutes to set.

4. Meanwhile, fit a large Dutch oven with a thermometer, then add the oil. Heat over medium heat to 350°F.

5. Working in batches, gently lower 4 or 5 shrimp into the oil. Cook, flipping a few times, until nicely golden brown all over, 2 to 3 minutes. Transfer the shrimp to the paper towels to drain. Return the oil to 350°F, then add the next batch and repeat.

6. Arrange the shrimp on a platter with the dip and serve immediately.

Gold Rush Wings

Serves 6 to 8

My love for honey mustard has been a lifelong affair that began with chicken nuggets and dipping sauce and eventually fixated on these sweet and spicy gold rush wings. A mix of honey, mustard, and Frank's hot sauce gives them their beautiful golden coat and deeply addictive flavor. Baking the wings means I can get a large batch tossed in the sauce when they're still hot without losing that greasy, tender joy of a perfect wing. These are flavor-packed, finger-licking, and impossible not to love!

SAUCE

4 tablespoons (½ stick) unsalted butter, melted

½ cup honey

½ cup yellow mustard

¼ cup Frank's RedHot or hot sauce of your choice

½ teaspoon kosher salt

½ teaspoon garlic powder

½ teaspoon onion powder

½ teaspoon smoked paprika

WINGS

5 pounds chicken wings, tips removed, drumettes and flats separated

2 tablespoons neutral oil

1 tablespoon kosher salt

1 teaspoon freshly ground black pepper

½ teaspoon baking soda

3 tablespoons toasted sesame seeds

1. Place the racks in the upper and lower third of the oven and preheat to 425°F. Line two rimmed sheet pans with foil and set a wire rack over each.

2. **MAKE THE SAUCE:** In a medium bowl, whisk the butter, honey, mustard, hot sauce, salt, garlic powder, onion power, and paprika.

3. **MAKE THE WINGS:** Pat the wings dry with paper towels. In a large bowl, combine the neutral oil, salt, black pepper, and baking soda. Add the wings toss to coat well.

4. Divide the wings between the prepared sheet pans, arranging them in a single layer. Bake for 45 to 50 minutes, swapping racks and rotating the sheets halfway through, until the wings are golden brown and the skin is crisp.

5. Just before the wings finish, pour ¾ cup of the sauce into a separate large bowl. When they finish baking, immediately transfer the wings to the bowl and toss to coat in the sauce. Add 2 tablespoons of the sesame seeds and toss again.

6. Stack the wings on a serving platter and sprinkle the remaining 1 tablespoon sesame seeds on top. Pour the remaining sauce into a small bowl for dipping and serve immediately.

Puttin' On the Ritz Crab Dip

Serves 6 to 8

The phrase to "put on the ritz" means to dress or present oneself as fancy or fashionable, but if I am being honest, nothing is fancier or more fashionable to me than a rich, buttery Ritz cracker. They make pretty much everything better, and, here, they are the crown jewel in my simple, spicy, and creamy crab dip. Calabrian chili paste is my preferred addition for heat, but any hot sauce will do the job, or you can leave it out. For entertaining a crowd, it's worth the Ritz.

Make Ahead *The cooked and cooled crab mixture can be covered with cling wrap and refrigerated up to 24 hours.*

Nonstick cooking spray

3 tablespoons unsalted butter

2 celery stalks, diced

1 green bell pepper, diced

1 shallot, minced

2 garlic cloves, minced

1 tablespoon Calabrian chili paste

1 tablespoon Worcestershire sauce

1½ teaspoons kosher salt

½ teaspoon freshly ground black pepper

1 tablespoon all-purpose flour

½ cup whole milk

8 ounces cream cheese

8 ounces lump crabmeat

6 scallions, thinly sliced

1 sleeve Ritz crackers (32 crackers), lightly crushed

Toasted baguette slices, for serving

1. Preheat the oven to 400°F. Coat a 1-quart baking dish, pie plate, or oven-safe skillet with nonstick spray.

2. Melt the butter in a large skillet over medium heat. Add the celery, bell pepper, shallot, and garlic. Cook, stirring occasionally, until the vegetables are fragrant and beginning to soften, about 3 minutes. Add the Calabrian chili paste, Worcestershire, salt, and black pepper, then stir in the flour until the mixture is thick. Stir in the milk, then add the cream cheese and stir to melt, about 3 minutes. Remove the skillet from the heat and fold in the crabmeat and half the scallions.

3. Scrape the mixture into the prepared baking dish. Blanket the top with the crushed crackers. Bake for 15 to 20 minutes, until the crackers are lightly browned and the dip is bubbling around the edges. Let sit for 10 minutes, then sprinkle on the remaining scallions before serving with baguette slices alongside.

Nachos Grossy

Serves 6 to 8

When you order nachos grande at a restaurant, you expect *the works*. Nachos Grossy delivers all of that to you at home—the abundance of restaurant nachos minus *the work*. This is the perfect throw-together recipe for a lot of people, with a vibrant pico that can be made ahead and quick-seared steak that gets a citrus soak. Building my ideal tray is all about layering the condiments, cheese, and toppings so every bite has a big impact. And while we are making these nachos at home, I stick to restaurant-style tortilla chips, as they are typically larger (for holding more cheese) and crispier (more crunch).

Make Ahead *The pico and seared steaks in marinade can be refrigerated in separate airtight containers up to 24 hours.*

PICO

1 jalapeño, roughly chopped

½ medium red onion, roughly chopped

2 garlic cloves

¼ cup fresh cilantro leaves

Juice of 1 lime

Kosher salt and freshly ground black pepper

2 vine tomatoes, roughly chopped

STEAK

2 pounds skirt steak

Kosher salt and freshly ground black pepper

2 garlic cloves, grated

Zest and juice of 2 limes

Juice of 1 orange

2 tablespoons neutral oil

NACHOS

¼ cup sour cream

Juice of 1 lime

1 tablespoon hot sauce, such as Cholula

2 (12-ounce) bags tortilla chips

2 (15.5-ounce) cans pinto beans, drained and rinsed

16 ounces pepper Jack cheese, shredded

16 ounces Colby Jack cheese, shredded

2 jalapeños, thinly sliced (optional)

1 avocado, halved, pitted, peeled, and sliced

¼ cup fresh cilantro leaves

2 scallions, thinly sliced

1. Preheat the oven to 400°F.

2. **MAKE THE PICO:** In a food processor, combine the jalapeño, onion, garlic, cilantro, lime juice, and a good pinch each of salt and pepper. Pulse 4 to 5 times, until finely chopped. Add the tomatoes and pulse about 4 more times, until diced. (Alternatively, finely chop everything by hand.) Taste and add more salt and pepper as needed, then cover tightly with cling wrap and refrigerate until ready to use, up to 24 hours.

3. **MAKE THE STEAK:** Pat the steaks dry with paper towels, then generously season all over with salt and pepper. In a zip-top bag, combine the garlic, lime zest, lime juice, and orange juice.

4. Heat the oil in a large cast-iron skillet over high heat until just smoking. Add the steaks and cook until charred on the outside, about 2 minutes per side. Immediately transfer the steaks to the citrus mixture to marinate for 10 minutes.

5. **MEANWHILE, MAKE THE NACHOS:** In a small bowl, whisk the sour cream, lime juice, and hot sauce.

6. On a rimmed sheet pan, evenly spread out one bag of the tortilla chips. Sprinkle half the pinto beans over the top, then cover with half the pepper Jack and Colby Jack cheeses. Cut the steak against the grain into bite-size pieces and lay half of it over the cheese, then finish with half the jalapeño slices (if using). Repeat the process with the remaining chips, beans, cheese, steak, and jalapeño.

7. Bake for about 10 minutes, until the cheese is melted and everything is warmed through. Immediately spoon the pico evenly over the top, then drizzle with the sour cream mixture. Finish with avocado, cilantro, and scallions before serving.

Pineapple Fennel Pulled Pork Sliders

Serves 6 to 8

Sliders are famously a two-bite delight. *These* sliders are so delicious, I think we can get that down to one bite. The pork braises slowly for hours in a homemade barbecue sauce featuring layers of smoky, tangy notes, along with large pieces of fennel for a subtle anise flavor and sweet chunks of pineapple. Each bite is a perfect mix of flavors and textures, from the rich, fall-apart pork to the crunchy bread and butter pickles, and soft Hawaiian rolls. These sliders can slide into my DMs for an invite anytime!

Make Ahead *The shredded, cooled pork can be covered with cling wrap and refrigerated up to 3 days.*

BEER BARBECUE SAUCE

2 teaspoons neutral oil

1 medium red onion, diced

½ teaspoon kosher salt

12 ounces brown or amber ale

½ cup ketchup

¼ cup packed dark brown sugar

¼ cup honey

2 tablespoons soy sauce

2 tablespoons apple cider vinegar

2 teaspoons garlic powder

2 teaspoons smoked paprika

1 teaspoon ground cumin

1 teaspoon freshly ground black pepper

SLIDERS

2 tablespoons neutral oil

2 pounds pork shoulder

Kosher salt and freshly ground black pepper

1 large fennel bulb, halved and thinly sliced

16 ounces frozen pineapple, thawed

2 (12-count) packages Hawaiian sweet rolls

Bread and butter pickles, for serving

1. **MAKE THE SAUCE:** Heat the oil in a small saucepan over medium heat. When the oil is shimmering, add the onion and salt. Cook, stirring occasionally, until softened, about 5 minutes. Add the beer, ketchup, brown sugar, honey, soy sauce, vinegar, garlic powder, paprika, cumin, and black pepper. Bring to a simmer, stirring often, then cook until the sauce is slightly thickened and the flavors have melded, about 10 minutes.

2. **MAKE THE SLIDERS:** In a large Dutch oven, heat the oil over medium-high heat. Season the pork generously with salt and pepper. When the oil is shimmering, add the pork and cook until browned, about 5 minutes per side.

3. Add the fennel, pineapple, and barbecue sauce. Stir to mix, then cover and reduce the heat to low. Simmer until the pork is very tender, about 3 hours. About 15 minutes before the pork is done, remove the lid and increase the heat to high. Cook, stirring often, until the sauce is reduced by about a third and thickly coats the pork, about 15 minutes. Remove from the heat. Use two forks to shred the pork in the pan and toss to coat in the sauce. Let cool for 10 minutes.

4. Use a serrated knife to cut through the sheet of rolls crosswise, leaving the bottoms and the tops connected. Lay the bottoms on a serving platter and spoon the pulled pork on top. Arrange the pickles all over the pork, then press the tops down to close the sandwiches before serving. Let everyone reach in to pull the rolls apart.

Caramelized Banana Pudding

Serves 6 to 8

From the boxed mixes of my childhood to a deep love of Magnolia Bakery, it's safe to say banana pudding is one of my favorite desserts. This version is the adult makeover of that childhood favorite. We're taking everything up a notch with sugar-cinnamon-coated bananas caramelized in the oven and a tangy addition of Greek yogurt to the pudding and whipped cream. But don't worry, adults can still experience the joys of childhood—namely boxed vanilla pudding and Nilla Wafers, who are still the stars here, because why mess with perfection? It's a dream make-ahead dessert for hosting, because it needs lots of fridge time so all the flavors, old and new, can get to know one another.

Make Ahead The assembled pudding can be refrigerated up to 24 hours.

---

8 ripe bananas

½ cup packed dark brown sugar

Ground cinnamon

2 (5-ounce) packages instant vanilla pudding

4 cups half-and-half, very cold

2 (14-ounce) cans sweetened condensed milk

2 cups heavy cream, very cold

¼ cup plain full-fat Greek yogurt

2 (11-ounce) boxes Nilla wafers

I. Place a rack 6 inches from the broiler heat source and preheat the broiler. Line a rimmed sheet pan with parchment paper or foil.

2. Peel the bananas and cut each one in half crosswise, then lengthwise, to create four pieces. Arrange them on the prepared sheet pan (or use two), cut sides up. Sprinkle the brown sugar evenly over the bananas and finish with a few good shakes of cinnamon. Broil until the sugar is caramelized, 5 to 7 minutes, turning halfway through. Let cool completely on the sheet pan, about 30 minutes.

3. In a large bowl, whisk the vanilla pudding and half-and-half until thick, about 2 minutes. Whisk in the sweetened condensed milk. In a separate large bowl, combine the heavy cream and yogurt. Using a handheld mixer on medium, whisk until stiff peaks form, about 4 minutes. Reserve 2 cups of the whipped cream, then fold the remainder into the pudding until no streaks remain.

4. Build three layers of pudding: Start with half a package of Nilla Wafers on the bottom (they'll pile up!), then layer about a third of the bananas and a third of the pudding. Repeat 2 more times, using all the bananas and pudding.

5. Crumble the remaining half package of Nilla wafers and sprinkle on top, then scoop on the reserved whipped cream. Refrigerate for at least 4 hours before serving.

Spring Awakening

Make THE *Menu*

● **1 DAY BEFORE**

A Simple Green Salad with Shallot Dressing: Make the dressing and wash the greens. Store separately in the fridge.

Lamb Chops with Tangy Apricot Sauce: Marinate the lamb and store in the fridge.

Spinach & Artichoke Dip Pasta Bake: Assemble the pasta and store in the fridge.

● **MORNING OF**

Roasted Asparagus with Parmesan Sauce: Trim the asparagus and store in the fridge.

Spinach & Artichoke Dip Pasta Bake: Make the pita topping.

AFTER A LONG WINTER OF HIBERNATION,

the early waves of fresh produce and warm sunshine mark the true awakening of the year for me. We start rearranging our closets, swapping out our purses, and asking everyone we know if we should try bangs. The days are getting longer, and the landscape is exploding in green. Spring is in the air—you can smell it!

It's also my last chance for warm, cozy cooking before the humidity starts creeping in. There's a special pleasure in preparing meals that bring together the richness of winter and the lightness of spring, offering the best of both. These recipes bridge the gap between hearty comfort and fresh, vibrant flavors. We're celebrating the season's best ingredients to help you make the most of spring's abundance and look forward to those long, sunny days ahead!

● **2 HOURS BEFORE**

Chicken Thighs with Peas & Mom's Rice: Make the chicken and rice. Cover to keep warm.

● **1 HOUR BEFORE**

Spinach & Artichoke Dip Pasta Bake: Bake the pasta and cover to keep warm.

Olive Oil & Pistachio Berry Crisp: Assemble the filling and topping and store in the fridge.

● **15 MINUTES BEFORE**

Roasted Asparagus with Parmesan Sauce: Make the asparagus and Parm sauce. Keep warm separately.

A Simple Green Salad with Shallot Dressing: Assemble the salad.

Lamb Chops with Tangy Apricot Sauce: Cook the lamb chops and make apricot sauce. Arrange on a platter.

● **SERVING TIME**

Roasted Asparagus with Parmesan Sauce: Spoon the Parm sauce over the asparagus.

Olive Oil & Pistachio Berry Crisp: Bake the crisp for dessert.

A Simple Green Salad *with* Shallot Dressing

Serves 6 to 8

Inspired by the giant green salads at two of my favorite produce-driven restaurants, Stissing House in Pine Plains, New York, and Via Carota in Manhattan's West Village, this recipe is, for me, about the simplicity of getting some greens on the dinner table. It's really just a pile of lettuce greens and an easy-to-make dressing, but it still feels like a celebration of spring. I use a mix of whatever looks great at the market (watercress, dandelion greens, frisée, chicory, or beet greens would swap in brilliantly); this light, sweet shallot vinaigrette is perfect no matter what it's on.

Make Ahead The dressing can be refrigerated in an airtight container up to 3 days.

1 large shallot, finely minced

1 garlic clove, grated

2 tablespoons white wine vinegar

½ cup extra-virgin olive oil

2 teaspoons Dijon mustard

2 teaspoons honey

Kosher salt and freshly ground black pepper

1 romaine heart, trimmed and rinsed (see Note)

1 head butter lettuce, trimmed and rinsed (see Note)

1 head endive, trimmed and rinsed (see Note)

1. In a small bowl, combine the shallot, garlic, and vinegar. Set aside for 10 minutes to let the flavors mellow. Whisk in the olive oil, mustard, honey, and a generous pinch each of salt and pepper. Taste for seasoning and add more salt and pepper as needed.

2. In a large, shallow serving bowl, arrange a layer of mixed greens, spoon some dressing over the top, and add a few cranks of pepper. Keep building your salad, going for lots of height and drama, layering up the rest of the greens and dressing. Serve immediately.

Note

To clean the greens, cut the root off each bunch so the leaves are easy to separate. Rinse in plenty of cold water to get any dirt off, then dry thoroughly in a salad spinner or spread in an even layer on a clean kitchen towel to air dry. Once dry, the dried leaves can be wrapped in fresh paper towels and refrigerated in a zip-top bag up to 3 days.

Roasted Asparagus *with* Parmesan Sauce

Serves 6 to 8

When I studied abroad in Rome, my curriculum was supposed to be focused on architecture, but the education I actually took home was how good down-to-earth authentic Italian cooking could be. One of the most memorable things I ate that year was asparagus simply topped with grated Parmesan. That's it! That's all it needed to be perfect. Since asparagus is one the stars of the spring season, I like quickly roasting until it's perfectly tender and then spooning on this light spring jacket of a Parmesan sauce. And while I personally only wear a light spring jacket one or two days out of the year, I find this sauce gets worn much more frequently.

I large bunch asparagus, trimmed

Extra-virgin olive oil

Kosher salt

½ lemon

I tablespoon unsalted butter

I tablespoon all-purpose flour

¾ cup heavy cream

¼ cup freshly grated Parmesan cheese

Freshly ground black pepper

I. Preheat the oven to 450°F.

2. Arrange the asparagus on a rimmed sheet pan in an even layer. Drizzle on some olive oil, season with salt, and roll them to coat well.

3. Roast the asparagus until tender, I0 to I5 minutes. Remove from the oven and transfer to a serving platter. Squeeze the lemon juice over top.

4. In a small saucepan, melt the butter over medium heat. Whisk in the flour, and cook until lightly toasted, about I minute. Slowly add the cream, whisking constantly to avoid lumps. Add the Parmesan and a pinch of salt. Cook, whisking constantly, until the sauce is thickened, about 3 minutes. Taste for seasoning and add more salt as needed.

5. Spoon the sauce over the asparagus and finish with lots of pepper before serving.

Note
The asparagus can also be grilled over high heat for about 3 minutes on each side.

Spinach & Artichoke Dip Pasta Bake

Serves 6 to 8

Spinach and artichoke dip is my ultimate snack (shout-out to my Hillstone Girlies! IYKYK)—so briny, cheesy, and gooey. In my grand tradition of turning food I love into more food I love, I decided to transform the perfect dip into the perfect pasta. All that richness is the ideal base for a baked pasta dish, making for lots of beautiful cheese pulls and keeping everything creamy-dreamy in the oven. To honor its origins as a dip, a topping of crushed and seasoned pita chips adds a perfect crunchy texture to every bite.

Make Ahead: The pasta can be assembled in the baking dish, cooled, covered with cling wrap, and refrigerated up to 24 hours; bring to room temperature before baking.

Kosher salt

1 pound dried mezze rigatoni or rigatoni pasta

¼ cup extra-virgin olive oil, plus more for the pasta

2 cups plain pita chips

Zest and juice of 1 lemon

1 cup freshly grated Parmesan cheese

1 medium yellow onion, diced

2 scallions, sliced

1 teaspoon ground nutmeg

½ teaspoon garlic powder

Freshly ground black pepper

2 (8-ounce) bags fresh baby spinach

2 (14-ounce) cans quartered artichoke hearts, drained

8 ounces cream cheese, at room temperature

1 cup whole milk

2 cups shredded mozzarella cheese

1. Preheat the oven to 400°F.

2. Bring a large Dutch oven of salted water to a boil over high heat. Add the pasta and cook until al dente according to the package directions. Reserve 1 cup of the pasta cooking water, then drain. Toss the pasta with a drizzle of olive oil to prevent sticking.

3. Meanwhile, roughly crush the pita chips into a medium bowl. Add the lemon zest and ¼ cup of the Parmesan. Toss to mix well.

4. Wipe the Dutch oven dry. Add the olive oil and set over medium heat. When the oil is shimmering, add the onion. Cook, stirring occasionally, until translucent, about 5 minutes. Stir in the scallions, nutmeg, garlic powder, and a big pinch each of salt and pepper. Working in batches, add the spinach and stir to wilt. When all the spinach is in the pot, add the artichokes, cream cheese, milk, and ½ cup of reserved pasta cooking water. Cook, stirring often, until the sauce is thickened, about 5 minutes.

5. Remove from the heat and add the pasta, lemon juice, 1 cup of the mozzarella, and the remaining ¾ cup Parmesan. Stir until the pasta is coated and the cheese is melted, adding additional splashes of pasta water as needed. Taste for seasoning and add more salt as needed. Smooth into an even layer.

6. Sprinkle the remaining 1 cup mozzarella over the top, then add the pita mixture. Bake for 20 to 30 minutes, until the top is crisp and the sauce is bubbling. Serve immediately.

Lamb Chops *with* Tangy Apricot Sauce

Serves 6 to 8

Bimpy and Grandma Katherine always hosted Easter dinner at their house. Every year the showstopper was a big rack of lamb. And every year, as Bimpy was carving that rack at the table, he would pull out his favorite line: "I shoulda been a surgeon!" I'll leave the rack jokes, and theatrical carving, to Bimpy, and instead make these easy, individual marinated chops. After resting overnight in a mix of mustard and herbs, the chops sear in a matter of minutes. Then, while they take a rest, I use the same skillet to whip up a quick, tart apricot sauce to spoon over. And while it may not be the rack of Bimpy's dreams, it's all the same impressive taste with zero hassle.

Make Ahead: The lamb can marinate in the fridge up to 24 hours.

¼ cup extra-virgin olive oil

2 tablespoons Dijon mustard

2 tablespoons chopped fresh rosemary

2 tablespoons chopped fresh oregano

1 tablespoon fresh thyme leaves

Kosher salt

½ teaspoon red pepper flakes

2 pounds bone-in lamb rib chops, about 8 pieces

1 tablespoon neutral oil

1 tablespoon red wine vinegar

1 pound apricots, pitted and quartered

1. In a large zip-top bag or airtight container, combine the olive oil, mustard, rosemary, oregano, thyme, 2 teaspoons salt, and the pepper flakes. Seal and shake to mix the ingredients. Add the chops and turn to coat. Seal and marinate in the fridge for at least 4 hours or up to 24 hours.

2. Heat the neutral oil in a large nonstick skillet over medium heat. When the oil just begins to smoke, add the chops, working in batches as needed. Cook until browned on the outside and medium-rare in the center, about 2 minutes per side (or 3 minutes for well done). Transfer the chops to a serving platter and set aside to rest.

3. Immediately add the vinegar to the hot skillet and scrape up any browned bits from the bottom. Add the apricots and cook until barely soft, about 1 minute. Season with a pinch of salt, then spoon the mixture over the chops. Serve immediately.

Chicken Thighs *with* Peas & Mom's Rice

My mom's side of the family is both Italian and Portuguese. When it was her turn to cook dinner when I was growing up, she would often pull out her Portuguese specialties. One of my favorites was her Portuguese rice, bright red and super flavorful from the tomato paste and smoked paprika. She always made hers with linguiça, a smoked pork sausage that can be a tad hard to find. I prefer skipping it in favor of using the rice as the base for one-pot meals—this one stars chicken, peas, and rice.

Serves 8

2 tablespoons extra-virgin olive oil

8 boneless, skinless chicken thighs, cut into 1-inch pieces

1 large red bell pepper, diced

1 large white onion, diced

1½ teaspoons kosher salt

1½ teaspoons freshly ground black pepper

1 tablespoon smoked paprika

½ teaspoon red pepper flakes

1 (6-ounce) can or (4-ounce) tube tomato paste

3 cups low-sodium chicken broth

1 cup long-grain white rice, rinsed

2 dried bay leaves

1 cup fresh or frozen peas

Chopped fresh parsley, for serving

1. Preheat the oven to 350°F.

2. Heat the olive oil in a large Dutch oven over medium heat. When the oil is shimmering, add the chicken thighs, bell pepper, onion, salt, and black pepper. Cook, stirring often, until the vegetables are soft and the outside of the chicken is no longer pink, about 5 minutes, then stir in the paprika and pepper flakes. Immediately stir in the tomato paste and cook until it thickens and turns a deep red color, about 3 minutes. Pour in the chicken broth and scrape up any browned bits from the bottom of the pot. Stir in the rice and bay leaves. Bring the mixture to a rolling boil, then cover and transfer to the oven.

3. Bake for 35 to 40 minutes, until the liquid is almost all absorbed and the rice and chicken are cooked through. Remove from the oven, uncover, and sprinkle the peas over the top. Cover again and let sit for 10 minutes so the peas can cook and the rice can become extra creamy.

4. Remove the lid and give a gentle stir to mix the peas and fluff the rice. Garnish with plenty of parsley just before serving from the pot.

CHICKEN THIGHS WITH
PEAS & MOM'S RICE,
PAGE 229

Olive Oil & Pistachio Berry Crisp

Serves 6 to 8

Let's be honest, I make a fruit crisp twelve months a year with whatever fruit I have on hand. But fresh spring berries are where this dessert truly shines. To celebrate them, this updated crisp topping has a nutty, peppery flavor thanks to the chopped pistachios and olive oil, giving it a unique and almost savory edge. And, of course, the combination of gooey, sweet filling and crunchy topping is where the magic really happens. Whether you use a mix of berries or stick to one type, this crisp is a delicious celebration of spring and the annual kick-off to peak fruit crisp season!

FILLING

1 pound fresh strawberries, stemmed and halved or quartered

1 pint fresh blueberries

1 pint fresh blackberries

6 tablespoons granulated sugar

Zest and juice of 1 lemon

2 tablespoons all-purpose flour

TOPPING

1 cup all-purpose flour

1 cup rolled oats

¾ cup packed dark brown sugar

½ cup granulated sugar

½ cup chopped raw pistachios

1 teaspoon kosher salt

½ cup extra-virgin olive oil, plus more for serving

4 tablespoons (½ stick) unsalted butter, cubed

FOR SERVING

Greek yogurt

Honey

Vanilla ice cream

Extra-virgin olive oil

1. Preheat the oven to 350°F.

2. **MAKE THE FILLING:** In a large cast-iron skillet or 8-inch square baking pan, toss the berries with the granulated sugar, lemon zest and juice, and flour. Spread into an even layer.

3. **MAKE THE TOPPING:** In a medium bowl, stir together the flour, oats, brown sugar, granulated sugar, pistachios, and salt. Add the olive oil and butter and pinch to form a soft crumbly mixture. Sprinkle it evenly over the top of the filling. Set the skillet on a rimmed sheet pan.

4. Bake for about 1 hour, until the filling is bubbling and thick and the topping is golden brown all over. Let cool for about 30 minutes to let the juices settle and the filling set.

5. Serve big scoops of crisp with a dollop of Greek yogurt and a drizzle of honey on top or go all in with a scoop of vanilla ice cream and a drizzle of olive oil!

My *Mug* Runneth Over

Make THE Menu

● **2 DAYS BEFORE**

Grapefruit Mule: Make the mint syrup and store in the fridge.

Magic Seven-Layer Sundae Bar: Make the chocolate sauce and butterscotch sauce. Store separately in the fridge.

● **1 DAY BEFORE**

Mozzarella Sticks with (Drinkable) Marinara: Make the marinara and store in the fridge.

A Very Green Minestrone: Make the minestrone and store in the fridge.

One-Pot Broccoli, Shells & Cheese: Make the broccoli mixture and store in the fridge.

I SPENT MY FIRST THREE YEARS IN NEW YORK CITY

in a tiny studio apartment in the West Village that had an even tinier kitchen. Despite the size, some of my best memories and meals came out of that place. There wasn't much room for entertaining—I didn't have a dining table, and I barely had any counter space. But I did have a small sofa, two chairs, a couple of stools, and a coffee table. So when I hosted dinner parties, everyone found a seat and got comfy. But if you've ever tried balancing a fork, a plate, a napkin, and a drink while sitting on the floor or the arm of a sofa, you know it's quite the challenge. That's how I got the idea for a mug party. As in, mug in one hand, fork in the other—no balancing act required.

Everywhere I've lived (including that apartment), I've had a cabinet filled with an eclectic mug collection from all different chapters of my life. So I had plenty of mugs to go around and started creating recipes that could easily be eaten from a mug—mainly scoopable things like soups, pastas, and ice cream—to streamline a dinner party without a dinner table. Between courses, my guests would bring their mugs to the world's smallest sink, give them a quick rinse, and get ready for the next dish. Even now, with more than enough space for hosting, I still love the idea of a mug party as a charming way to enjoy a meal with friends, plus my mug collection has only gotten bigger . . .

● **1 HOUR BEFORE**

Mozzarella Sticks with (Drinkable) Marinara: Form the mozzarella sticks and freeze.

Magic Seven-Layer Sundae Bar: Make the coconut whipped cream and store in the fridge.

● **15 MINUTES BEFORE**

Mozzarella Sticks with (Drinkable) Marinara: Reheat the marinara and cook the mozzarella sticks.

One-Pot Broccoli, Shells & Cheese: Make the pasta and sauce.

A Very Green Minestrone: Reheat the minestrone.

Grapefruit Mule: Mix the punch and set out garnishes.

● **SERVING TIME**

Magic Seven-Layer Sundae Bar: Reheat the chocolate sauce and butterscotch sauce, re-whip the coconut whipped cream, and set out the garnishes for dessert.

4

Mozzarella Sticks *with* (Drinkable) Marinara

Serves 6 to 8

Whenever Gus and I are trying a new restaurant, he knows *the gasp* means I've spotted mozzarella sticks on the menu. Honestly, who wouldn't light up at the sight of such golden, gooey delights? At home, after breading and frying your mozzarella sticks (really just string cheese in drag) you simply fill everyone's mugs with a little sweet-and-tangy marinara sauce. After the sticks run out, go ahead and sip on the rest of your sauce. Bimpy will be so proud!

Make Ahead The marinara can be refrigerated in an airtight container up to 3 days.

(DRINKABLE) MARINARA
1 (14.5-ounce) can diced tomatoes

1 basil sprig

2 garlic cloves

Kosher salt and freshly ground black pepper

MOZZARELLA STICKS
½ cup all-purpose flour

3 large eggs

1½ cups panko breadcrumbs

½ cup freshly grated Parmesan cheese, plus more for serving

1 teaspoon kosher salt

½ teaspoon garlic powder

½ teaspoon dried oregano

12 sticks string cheese

2 quarts neutral oil

1. **MAKE THE MARINARA:** In a blender or food processor, combine the tomatoes, basil, garlic, and season with salt and pepper. Blend on medium speed until smooth, about 1 minute. Pour into a small saucepan and simmer over medium heat until thickened and reduced by half, about 10 minutes. Remove from the heat.

2. **MEANWHILE, MAKE THE MOZZARELLA STICKS:** Line a rimmed sheet pan with parchment paper. In a shallow bowl, evenly spread out the flour. In a second shallow bowl, beat the eggs. In a third shallow bowl, combine the panko, Parmesan, salt, garlic powder, and oregano.

3. Working with one at a time, roll a stick of string cheese through the flour to coat. Then roll it through the egg, allowing the excess to drip off, then toss it in the panko mixture, pressing gently to adhere. Roll it in the egg again, then the panko again. Set the coated mozzarella sticks on the prepared sheet pan. When all the sticks are in costume, freeze for 1 hour to set the coating.

4. Fit a large Dutch oven with a thermometer, then add the oil. Heat over medium-high heat to 400°F. Set a wire rack over a rimmed sheet pan.

5. Working in batches of 4 or 5, gently lower the mozzarella sticks into the oil. Cook, flipping occasionally, until golden brown all over, about 2 minutes. Transfer the mozzarella sticks to the wire rack. Return the oil to 400°F between each batch.

6. Warm the marinara over low heat, then ladle into mugs for dipping. Stack the mozzarella sticks in the mugs and dust with Parmesan before serving.

A Very Green Minestrone

Serves 6 to 8

After years working in the design world, I have a deep respect for a curated color palette and a sharp, fresh point of view. This green minestrone has both: it's green (shocking, I know) and tastes like an explosion of spring bounty in a bowl . . . or, in this case, a mug. But the overload of vibrant veggies and fresh herbs isn't just a feast for your eyes, it's also a hug for your taste buds.

Make Ahead The finished minestrone can be cooled, covered, and refrigerated up to 24 hours. Reheat over low heat just before serving.

Kosher salt

I cup dried ditalini or other small pasta

3 tablespoons extra-virgin olive oil

½ medium head green cabbage, thinly sliced (4 to 5 cups)

4 celery stalks, thinly sliced

2 garlic cloves, thinly sliced

Freshly ground black pepper

I large zucchini, diced

2 quarts vegetable broth

5 ounces fresh baby spinach

10 ounces frozen peas

Chopped fresh dill, parsley, and/or thinly sliced chives, for serving

1. Bring a large pot of salted water to a boil over high heat. Cook the pasta to al dente according to the package directions, then drain.

2. Meanwhile, heat the olive oil in a large Dutch oven over medium heat. When the oil is shimmering, add the cabbage, celery, garlic, and season with salt and pepper. Cook, stirring often, until the cabbage is softened, about 8 minutes.

3. Stir in the zucchini and cook until vibrant green, about 2 minutes. Add the vegetable broth and simmer until the flavors are melded, about 5 minutes. Add the spinach, peas, and cooked pasta. Stir until the spinach is wilted and everything is warmed through, about 2 minutes.

4. Finish the soup with a shower of dill, parsley, and/or chives just before serving.

One-Pot Broccoli, Shells & Cheese

Serves 6 to 8

As far as eating food on the couch goes, I don't think it's hard to imagine yourself as a kid, balancing a steaming bowl of shells and cheese on your blanket-covered lap. Each spoonful filled with that beloved came-from-a-box taste, likely because it did, in fact, come from a box. That same nostalgic taste (and ease) is in this one-pot wonder, but this time, we're thinking outside the box. A small pasta shape wrapped in a velvety, cheese sauce that is dotted with a confetti of broccoli, garlic, and Parmesan cheese. Of course, I use shells and bright orange cheddar to set the mood. It's almost as if that kid on the couch grew up to be an adult on the couch. Almost!

Make Ahead The broccoli mixture can be refrigerated in an airtight container up to 24 hours.

Kosher salt

1 pound dried medium shell pasta

1 medium head broccoli, cut into florets

½ cup freshly grated Parmesan cheese

3 garlic cloves

1 teaspoon freshly ground black pepper

½ teaspoon red pepper flakes

2 cups whole milk

2 tablespoons unsalted butter

1 pound orange cheddar cheese, grated

1. Bring a large pot of salted water to a boil over high heat. Add the shells and cook for 1 minute less than the package directions so they're extra al dente. Reserve 1 cup of the pasta cooking water, then drain.

2. Meanwhile, in a food processor, process the broccoli florets until finely chopped, about 2 minutes. Scrape down the sides and add the Parmesan, garlic, 1 teaspoon salt, the black pepper, and the pepper flakes. Process again until combined, about 1 minute more.

3. Return the pot from the pasta (no need to wipe it out) to medium heat. Add the milk and butter and bring to a gentle simmer, about 3 minutes. Add the broccoli mixture along with the cheddar cheese and cook, stirring constantly, until the cheese is fully melted and the sauce is simmering, about 3 minutes.

4. Add the pasta to the cheese sauce and stir until the pasta is thickly coated, about 2 minutes, adding splashes of the reserved pasta cooking water to help coat as needed. Taste for seasoning and add more salt as needed. Serve immediately.

Grapefruit Mule

Makes 8 drinks

This mocktail is a fresh twist on the classic Moscow Mule, perfect for waking up your guests' taste buds as they arrive. Served in a mug packed with ice, it features the zesty flavors of grapefruit juice, mint, and ginger beer. A little tart, a little sweet, a little bite from the ginger—it's guaranteed to make a perfect first impression.

Make Ahead The mint syrup can be refrigerated in an airtight container up to 1 month ahead.

6 (12-ounce) bottles ginger beer

2 cups Mint Syrup (recipe follows)

2 cups grapefruit juice

½ teaspoon kosher salt

FOR SERVING

Crushed ice

Mint sprigs

Lime wheels

In a large punch bowl or serving bowl, stir together the ginger beer, mint syrup, grapefruit juice, and salt. Pack mugs with ice and ladle in the punch. Garnish each with a mint sprig and lime wheel.

Mint Syrup

MAKES 2 CUPS

1⅔ cups sugar

2 cups fresh mint leaves

In a medium saucepan, combine the sugar and 1⅔ cups water. Bring to a boil over high heat, stirring occasionally to dissolve the sugar, then cook until the syrup thickens, about 5 minutes. Remove from the heat and stir in the mint leaves. Cover and let cool completely, about 2 hours. Discard the mint and transfer the syrup to an airtight container. Refrigerate until ready to use.

Magic Seven-Layer Sundae Bar

Serves 6 to 8

My grandma Katherine loved to make Magic Seven-Layer Bars, sometimes called Hello Dolly Bars, but, no matter how many times I try, I can never count seven layers. Graham crackers, shredded coconut, chopped walnuts, butterscotch chips, and chocolate chips (that's five!) all pile up and then get drenched in sweetened condensed milk (six . . .) that caramelizes as it bakes. The end result? Pure magic. I've taken those incredible flavors and transformed them into a seven-layer sundae. Each ingredient becomes a sundae topping to set out as a make-your-own bar, giving your guests the freedom to make their own sundaes with as many layers as they like. Let me know if you find lucky number seven!

Make Ahead *The chocolate and butterscotch sauces can be refrigerated in airtight containers up to 2 weeks.*

CHOCOLATE SAUCE

1½ cups granulated sugar

½ cup unsweetened cocoa powder

½ teaspoon kosher salt

1 cup whole milk

4 ounces semisweet chocolate, chopped

4 tablespoons (½ stick) unsalted butter, cubed

1 teaspoon pure vanilla extract

BUTTERSCOTCH SAUCE

½ cup (1 stick) unsalted butter

2 cups packed dark brown sugar

2 teaspoons kosher salt

1½ cups heavy cream

2 teaspoons pure vanilla extract

COCONUT WHIPPED CREAM

1 (13.5-ounce) can coconut cream, refrigerated overnight (see Note)

1 cup heavy cream

¼ cup powdered sugar

SUNDAES

1 cup chopped walnuts

1 cup sweetened coconut flakes

1 cup graham cracker crumbs

2 quarts vanilla ice cream

1. MAKE THE CHOCOLATE SAUCE: In a medium saucepan, whisk the granulated sugar, cocoa powder, and salt. Whisk in the milk, being sure to get the sides and bottom. Set over medium heat and bring to a simmer, whisking constantly, and cook until slightly thickened, about 5 minutes. Remove from the heat and add the chopped chocolate and butter. Whisk until completely melted, then whisk in the vanilla.

2. MAKE THE BUTTERSCOTCH SAUCE: In a medium saucepan, melt the butter over medium heat. Stir in the brown sugar and salt. Cook, stirring often, until the brown sugar goes from sandy to thick and bubbly, about 4 minutes. Slowly pour in the heavy cream—and step back as you pour because it'll bubble up and release steam, then calm down. Stir to incorporate. Simmer until the mixture reads 225°F on a thermometer, about 5 minutes. Remove from the heat and whisk in the vanilla.

3. MAKE THE COCONUT WHIPPED CREAM: Remove the can of coconut cream from the fridge and delicately open it; the refrigeration should have solidified the cream at the top. Use a small spoon to scoop the cream into a large bowl with the heavy cream and powdered sugar. Using a handheld mixer on medium speed, whip to stiff peaks, about 2 minutes. Cover the bowl tightly with cling wrap and refrigerate until ready to use, or up to 2 hours. Whip again for about 10 seconds before serving.

4. MAKE THE SUNDAES: Set out the chocolate sauce, butterscotch, coconut whipped cream, chopped walnuts, coconut flakes, and crushed graham crackers in bowls with serving spoons. Add a few scoops of ice cream to each person's mug and let them make their own magic with toppings.

Note

Coconut cream and cream of coconut are two different products.

The *Great* Outdoors

Make THE Menu

● **2 DAYS BEFORE**

Green Goddess Potato Salad: Make the potato salad and store in the fridge.

Carrot & Apple Slaw: Make the slaw and store in the fridge.

● **1 DAY BEFORE**

Turkey Clubs: Cook the bacon and make the sandwich spread. Store separately in the fridge.

Lobster Rolls: Make the lobster salad and store in the fridge.

Grilled Vegetable Sandwiches: Grill the vegetables and make the dressing. Store separately in the fridge.

I REMEMBER WATCHING EARLY EPISODES OF

Barefoot Contessa in which Ina would pack up a cooler for the beach or wrap up sandwiches to take on a picnic. She made eating outdoors seem easy, elegant, and approachable for me, the forever-indoors kid. If I *was* going to leave the house, I was going to do it the way a wealthy middle-aged woman with several gay friends would!

Cut to being wealthier, older, and with several gay friends around at all times (hey, checking three out of four boxes ain't bad) and now I appreciate the joy of packing up a Yeti tote with home-cooked goodies and meeting friends for an afternoon or evening alfresco. Eating outside connects you with your surroundings and slows down the meal. The trick is to focus on food that packs well, travels well, and can be served straight from the container. How do you know it's time to leave? When everybody's sweet tooth sets in, head to the nearest Mister Softee truck. Now grab your purse; we're going out to eat. Literally!

● **30 MINUTES BEFORE**

Carrot & Apple Slaw: Add the parsley leaves and toss.

Turkey Clubs: Toast the bread and assemble the sandwiches.

Lobster Rolls: Toast the rolls.

Grilled Vegetable Sandwiches: Toast the rolls and assemble the sandwiches.

● **SERVING TIME**

Lobster Rolls: Assemble the rolls.

Green Goddess Potato Salad

Serves 6 to 8

Ready to channel your inner goddess? This potato salad is all about going green, with creamy potatoes and tender veggies covered in a luscious, herby dressing. (The dressing is so good, you might want to make a double batch and stash some in the fridge!) It's the ultimate side dish for any picnic, barbecue, or weeknight dinner. Plus, it's a breeze to make ahead and equally tasty whether warm or chilled. The reactions you'll get to this dish are sure to make you feel like the culinary deity you are.

Make Ahead *The potato salad can be refrigerated in an airtight container up to 3 days.*

3 pounds baby potatoes, halved

Kosher salt

I bunch asparagus, trimmed and cut into I-inch pieces

8 ounces snap peas, cut into I-inch pieces

I cup frozen or fresh peas

Grossy Goddess Dressing (recipe follows)

½ cup chopped fresh dill

¼ cup finely chopped fresh chives

Freshly ground black pepper

I. Place the potatoes in a large Dutch oven and cover with 2 inches of cold water. Add a very generous amount of salt and bring to a boil over high heat. Cook until almost tender, about 8 minutes, then add the asparagus, snap peas, and peas. Continue cooking until the potatoes are knife-tender and the green vegetables are bright in color, about 2 minutes more. Drain and let cool for about 10 minutes.

2. Transfer the cooled potatoes and vegetables to a large bowl. Add the dressing, dill, chives, and lots of pepper. Toss to coat well, then taste for seasoning and add more salt and pepper as needed. Serve warm or cover with cling wrap and refrigerate until ready to serve, or up to 3 days.

Grossy Goddess Dressing

MAKES 1¾ CUPS

¾ cup sour cream

¾ cup mayonnaise

2 tablespoons fresh lemon juice

I cup fresh basil leaves

½ cup fresh parsley leaves

½ cup fresh mint leaves

3 anchovy fillets

2 garlic cloves

I tablespoon drained capers

I teaspoon kosher salt, plus more as needed

I teaspoon freshly ground black pepper, plus more as needed

½ teaspoon red pepper flakes, plus more as needed

In a blender, combine the sour cream, mayonnaise, lemon juice, basil, parsley, mint, anchovies, garlic, capers, salt, black pepper, and pepper flakes. Blend on high speed, stopping to scrape down the sides as needed, until fully combined, about 2 minutes. Taste for seasoning and add more salt, black pepper, or pepper flakes as needed. Use immediately or refrigerate in an airtight container for up to 3 days.

CARROT & APPLE SLAW, PAGE 250, AND GREEN GODDESS POTATO SALAD, PAGE 246

Carrot & Apple Slaw

Serves 6 to 8

This slaw is the epitome of warm-weather food. It's the kind of dish your mom and her friends would proudly bring to a picnic, but it's updated with fresh produce and flavors. It's both a nod to the past and a step into the present, which is exactly where I want my cooking to live. Make it ahead so the flavors have plenty of time to mix and mingle, then serve it nice and cold.

Make Ahead *The ungarnished slaw can be refrigerated in an airtight container up to 3 days.*

6 cups thinly sliced purple cabbage (from ½ large)

2 cups shredded carrots (from 2 large)

2 Granny Smith apples, peeled and cut into matchsticks

Kosher salt and freshly ground black pepper

¼ cup mayonnaise

2 tablespoons Dijon mustard

2 tablespoons apple cider vinegar

2 cups golden raisins

I cup fresh parsley leaves

In a large bowl, combine the cabbage, carrots, and apples. Season with salt and pepper and toss to mix. Add the mayonnaise, mustard, and vinegar and toss again to coat. Add the raisins and toss. Cover tightly with cling wrap and refrigerate for at least I hour or up to 3 days. Just before serving, add the parsley leaves and toss one more time.

Turkey Clubs

Makes 4 sandwiches

I'm a card-carrying member of the Turkey Club Club. It's a perfect sandwich under any circumstances, but most especially from hotel room service or every single diner that exists. Wrapped up tight and eaten in the sunshine? I do believe this may be peak turkey club. Crispy bacon, juicy tomatoes, and tender turkey in a triple decker stack on slices of toasty bread—and you can't forget the accompanying pickle. Personally, I always ask for a side of mustard to slather onto my sandwich for extra zing, and when I'm the chef, I do it my way, combining the mayo with two types of mustard and a splash of pickle juice for my dream sandwich spread. Welcome to the club!

Make Ahead The sandwich spread can be refrigerated in an airtight container up to 1 week.

8 slices thick-cut bacon

12 slices marble rye, sourdough, or whole wheat sandwich bread

Grossy's Sandwich Spread (recipe follows)

8 thick slices beefsteak tomatoes (from 2 large)

8 Bibb lettuce leaves

2 pounds deli turkey, sliced (see Note)

1. Preheat the oven to 450°F. Line a rimmed sheet pan with foil and set a wire rack on top.

2. Lay the bacon on the prepared rack. Bake for 10 to 15 minutes, until crispy. Leave the oven on; transfer the bacon to paper towels to drain. Once cool, snap the pieces in half.

3. Working in batches as needed, lay the bread slices on the same rack. Bake for 3 to 4 minutes on each side until toasted. Stack on a plate to cool.

4. Make one sandwich at a time: Slather the sandwich spread on one side of each of three slices of bread. On two of those slices, stack a tomato slice, a lettuce leaf, a few slices of turkey, and a piece of bacon. Layer the three slices to make a triple-decker sandwich. Insert toothpicks to hold the stack in place, then cut the sandwich into quarters. Repeat with the remaining ingredients to make four sandwiches.

5. Wrap them up and take them on the go!

Note
Ask your deli counter to slice the turkey about ⅛ inch thick, if possible.

Grossy's Sandwich Spread

MAKES ¾ CUP

¼ cup mayonnaise

¼ cup spicy brown mustard

3 tablespoons grainy mustard

1 tablespoon pickle juice

In a small bowl, whisk together the mayonnaise, both mustards, and the pickle juice. Use immediately or refrigerate in an airtight container for up to 1 week.

Lobster Rolls

Makes 4 sandwiches

People always want to know if I am a hot, buttery or cold, mayo-ey lobster roll person. I love them all, so my answer is always that I am simply "a lobster roll person." That said, when it comes to entertaining, I do have an opinion: I think a cold lobster salad dressed with mayo is the way to go. It's easy to make in advance and then heap into toasted, buttered buns, plus the addition of a lettuce leaf keeps the roll from getting soggy . . . not that they ever last that long, but just in case!

Make Ahead The lobster salad can be refrigerated in an airtight container up to 3 days.

I pound cooked lobster meat, chilled (see Note)

¼ cup mayonnaise, plus more as needed

2 tablespoons fresh lemon juice

2 tablespoons thinly sliced fresh chives, plus more for serving

½ teaspoon celery salt

½ teaspoon freshly ground black pepper

4 tablespoons (½ stick) unsalted butter

4 New England–style top-sliced or standard hot dog buns

4 Bibb lettuce leaves

1. In a medium bowl, stir together the lobster meat, mayonnaise, lemon juice, chives, celery salt, and pepper. Taste for seasoning and add another spoonful or two of mayo as you like.

2. Melt the butter in a large skillet over medium heat. Rub the sides and tops of the rolls in the melted butter, then toast, about 2 minutes per side. Set the rolls on a serving platter.

3. Pry the rolls open and lay a lettuce leaf in each one. Divide the lobster mixture evenly among the rolls, nestling it on top of the lettuce. Garnish each with a fresh sprinkle of chives before wrapping them up and heading out the door.

Note

A 1½-pound lobster will yield 6 to 8 ounces of meat. You can buy it already cooked and picked, but if you want to cook and crack your own, do so in a large pot of heavily salted water boiling over high heat until bright red, about 12 minutes.

LOBSTER ROLLS, PAGE 254

Grilled Vegetable Sandwiches

Makes 4 sandwiches

When it comes to vegetables in sandwiches, tomatoes and lettuce have been wildly (and understandably) over-served. But a pile of grilled vegetables charred to perfection and slapped between two slices of bread for a gorgeous sandwich makes me feel like I've won the lottery. With this recipe, I'm ready to share the winning ticket with you. I love a spread of goat cheese (the queen of all spreadable cheeses), the peppery bite of arugula, and a drizzle of vintage-yet-timeless creamy balsamic vinaigrette that soaks everything and makes each bite taste like a million bucks.

Make Ahead The dressing can be refrigerated in an airtight container up to 1 week. The cooled cooked vegetables can be refrigerated in an airtight container up to 3 days.

I large globe eggplant, cut lengthwise into 8 slices

2 large yellow squash, cut lengthwise into 4 slices each

2 red bell peppers, sliced into 5 pieces each

2 large red onions, sliced into 4 thick rounds each

I cup extra-virgin olive oil

Kosher salt and freshly ground black pepper

4 ciabatta rolls, split

2 cups baby arugula

Creamy Balsamic Dressing (recipe follows)

8 ounces goat cheese

1. Prepare the grill for medium heat (see page 65).

2. Generously brush the vegetables on one side with olive oil and season with salt and pepper. Working in batches, lay them oiled side down on the grill and cook until charred on the bottoms, about 5 minutes. Oil, salt, and pepper the top sides before flipping and grilling until charred on both sides, about 5 more minutes. Transfer to a plate.

3. Generously oil the insides of the ciabatta rolls. Grill until lightly toasted, 2 to 3 minutes.

4. In a medium bowl, toss the arugula with ¼ cup of the dressing.

5. Make an assembly line: Spread the goat cheese on the top halves of the rolls, dividing it evenly. Spread some creamy balsamic on the bottom halves. Divide the eggplant, yellow squash, bell pepper, and onion among the bottoms, then drizzle more dressing over the veggies. Finish with a small pile of arugula on each sandwich before pressing down the tops.

6. Wrap now, enjoy later.

Note
To make this recipe on the stove, use a preheated large cast-iron skillet over medium-high heat, coated with I tablespoon of neutral oil. Cook the vegetables in batches until golden brown and crisp, about 3 minutes per side. You can toast the rolls in the oil, too!

Creamy Balsamic Dressing

MAKES ¾ CUP

¼ cup balsamic vinegar

2 tablespoons mayonnaise

I tablespoon honey

I tablespoon Dijon mustard

½ teaspoon kosher salt

½ teaspoon garlic powder

½ teaspoon dried oregano

¼ cup extra-virgin olive oil

In a large bowl, whisk the vinegar, mayonnaise, honey, mustard, salt, garlic powder, and oregano. While vigorously whisking, very slowly drizzle in the olive oil, just a little bit at a time, until a creamy dressing forms. Use immediately or refrigerate in an airtight container for up to 1 week. Shake well before using after storage.

Grossy's Guide TAKE IT Outside

When the weather is gorgeous and it's time to pack the party to go, I do what I can to make the great outdoors feel like I live here now.

The Bare Necessities

As much as I want to pack a U-Haul and roll up to the park with my entire kitchen, I've learned that packing light is important and only to bring what I absolutely need:

SERVEWARE: Pack enough plates, cups, utensils, and napkins to cover everyone, then pack a few extra sets to be safe. I love packing up my enamelware plates and cups, everyday flatware, and cloth napkins to help the outdoors feel like an extension of my home.

CUTTING BOARD AND KNIFE: Bring along a small board and paring knife for slicing cheese, halving sandwiches, or cutting lemon or lime wedges for drinks. Even if you think you're all prepped, you'll be happy to have them.

CORKSCREW WITH BOTTLE OPENER: A must at every party, indoor or out.

WET WIPES: Every mom knows to keep the wipes within arm's reach. They're perfect for disinfecting, washing hands, wiping down plates, and swiping up spills.

PICNIC BLANKETS: I like to pack multiple lightweight blankets to scatter around. It creates a few different areas so everyone can mingle and move around.

TRASH BAG: Too many times I've been in a situation where the location either didn't have trash bins or the bins they did have were already overflowing. Bring a trash bag from home so you can carry everything back out with you. And bring an extra one for all the dirty plates, cups, and utensils you're going to wash when you get home.

SUNSCREEN AND BUG SPRAY: If I'm going outside, you can be sure I'm absolutely marinating in SPF and DEET.

Pack It Up!

You obviously need food, too! Your menu should be easy to transport, easy to assemble, and easy to eat. This is not the time to pull out the culinary stops. To take the meal on the go, we're going to need a few things:

ICE: To chill my cooler, I like to pack loose cubes in zip-top bags. They keep my food from getting wet, and then we can also use the ice for drinks later.

COOLER: Something big enough to comfortably fit all the food and ice, but not so big that hauling it becomes an Olympic event. I have various sizes for all events, from sturdy trunks to insulated bags. Layer the cooler with drinks and heavy containers at the bottom, delicate items at the top, and plenty of ice packs between each layer.

TOTE BAGS: For all the things that don't need to be chilled, like chips, crackers, and desserts. Blankets or cloth napkins can be tucked in here to help cushion and keep things snug. Pack a separate tote for all the other creature comforts you're bringing along, such as a sweatshirt or sunglasses. Bonus points if the bag's cute and functional—because we love a multitasker!

● HOW TO PACK...

SALADS OR SLICED FRUIT: Clean takeout containers, jars, or even zip-top bags. (I'm all about eating pasta salad straight out of the bag.)

DRESSINGS OR SAUCES: Store in mini airtight containers. Remember to give dressings a good shake before using.

SANDWICHES: Slice and wrap tightly in parchment paper or foil, like the little gifts they are.

CHEESE AND CHARCUTERIE: Keep them in their original packaging and arrange your board when you get there.

DESSERTS: Things like cookies, brownies, or bars can travel in a sturdy airtight container, stacked with layers of parchment to prevent sticking.

Nonna Your Business

Make THE Menu

● **2 DAYS BEFORE**

A Very Large Caesar Salad: Make the dressing and store in the fridge. Make the croutons and store at room temperature. Rinse and separate the lettuce leaves and store in the fridge.

Spicy (Enough) Arancini: Make the rice and store in the fridge.

Pork Chops with Vinegar Peppers: Season the pork chops and store in the fridge.

Struffoli: Make the dough and store in the fridge.

● **1 DAY BEFORE**

Lasagnetta: Assemble the lasagnetta and store in the fridge.

Nonna's Negroni: Brew the tea and store in the fridge.

SUNDAY SUPPER IS AN ITALIAN AMERICAN TRADITION, a weekly ritual in which family—and anyone else who shows up—gets stuffed to the brim. My dad and grandparents would tell stories of Sunday dinners past that had lasted for hours as they worked through course after course. Replicating magic like that is tough, but it won't stop me from trying.

At the core of all the entertaining I do, you know I'm channeling the energy of an Italian American grandmother—and that's the vibe we're serving here. A nonna has snacks on the table when you arrive and puts leftovers in your hands as you leave. Every minute in between, she'll be making sure you have everything you need and effortlessly warming your heart and belly. Channeling your inner nonna is all about caring for the people you love, making them feel at home, yelling across the table, sharing lots of laughs and a few heartaches (and maybe some heartburn). When you get everyone together for a classic Sunday supper, you can demand they show their love the Italian way: by cleaning their plate and asking for seconds!

● **MORNING OF**

Spicy (Enough) Arancini: Form into balls and store in the fridge.

Struffoli: Roll into balls and store in the fridge.

● **1 HOUR BEFORE**

Spicy (Enough) Arancini: Bread and cook. Keep warm in the oven.

Lasagnetta: Bake the lasagnetta. Keep warm in the oven.

● **30 MINUTES BEFORE**

Pork Chops with Vinegar Peppers: Make the pork chops and sauce.

● **15 MINUTES BEFORE**

Garlicky Broccoli Rabe: Make the broccoli rabe.

● **5 MINUTES BEFORE**

A Very Large Caesar Salad: Assemble the salad.

Nonna's Negroni: Mix the drink and set out garnishes.

● **SERVING TIME**

Pork Chops with Vinegar Peppers: Slice the pork and arrange on a platter.

Struffoli: Cook and assemble the struffoli for dessert.

A Very Large Caesar Salad

Serves 6 to 8

Size doesn't matter . . . unless we're talking about Caesar salad, that is. When it comes to this beloved salad, I want a huge bowl of it taking up space on the table, filled with whole leaves of crunchy romaine, big, chunky croutons, and long strips of Parmesan across the top. Most of all, I want a thick, salty, zippy dressing tossed in layer by layer, so no leaf goes naked.

Make Ahead *The dressing can be refrigerated in an airtight container up to 2 days. The toasted croutons can be stored in an airtight container at room temperature up to 2 days.*

DRESSING

½ cup freshly grated Parmesan cheese

6 anchovy fillets

2 large garlic cloves, grated

2 large egg yolks

Juice of ½ lemon, plus more as needed

2 teaspoons Dijon mustard

2 teaspoons freshly ground black pepper, plus more as needed

I teaspoon kosher salt, plus more as needed

½ cup extra-virgin olive oil

SALAD

I large loaf sourdough or crusty bread, cut into I-inch cubes

2 tablespoons extra-virgin olive oil

Kosher salt

2 romaine hearts, trimmed, rinsed, and leaves separated

I (8-ounce) block Parmesan cheese

Anchovy fillets, for serving (optional)

Freshly ground black pepper

I. Preheat the oven to 400°F.

2. **MAKE THE DRESSING:** In a blender, combine the Parmesan, anchovies, garlic, egg yolks, lemon juice, Dijon, pepper, and salt. Blend on low speed until combined, about I minute. With the blender running on low, very slowly drizzle in the olive oil just a little bit at a time until a thick dressing forms. Taste for seasoning and add more lemon juice, pepper, or salt as needed, then transfer to an airtight container and refrigerate while preparing the salad, or for up to 2 days.

3. **MAKE THE SALAD:** On a rimmed sheet pan, toss the bread with the olive oil and a pinch of salt. Bake for I5 minutes, flipping halfway through, until lightly toasted but not hard. Let cool on the sheet pan.

4. In a large bowl, combine a third of the leaves with a third of the dressing, then toss to coat well. Place in a serving bowl and use a vegetable peeler to peel large strips of Parmesan over the salad, then sprinkle a few croutons on top.

5. Continue to build the salad in the serving bowl, dressing the leaves and adding Parmesan and croutons in layers, using everything up. Lay a few anchovy fillets (if using) around the top of the salad, then finish with pepper. Serve immediately.

Spicy (Enough) Arancini

Makes 12 arancini

When Gus and I traveled to Sicily, the birthplace of arancini, my mouth was full of them 99 percent of the time. There were so many new flavor combinations to try, and naturally I felt it was my duty to taste them all. I think about them all the time, and I still can't get enough of the creamy, crispy risotto balls. (By the way, you could skip the frying and serve the base risotto right out of the pan as a perfect main.) I like a little spicy kick of Calabrian chili when I make them at home, just enough to make me break a sweat (not hard to do), but if you prefer them mild, just leave it out!

Make Ahead The cooled risotto can be covered with cling wrap and refrigerated up to 2 days.

RISOTTO
4 cups vegetable broth

2 tablespoons extra-virgin olive oil

1 cup Arborio rice

1 cup dry white wine

1 tablespoon Calabrian chili paste

½ teaspoon dried oregano

Kosher salt

2 tablespoons unsalted butter

1 tablespoon honey

ARANCINI
1 cup all-purpose flour

3 large eggs

1½ cups seasoned breadcrumbs

2 quarts neutral oil

Freshly grated Parmesan cheese, for serving

Red pepper flakes, for serving

1. **MAKE THE RISOTTO:** Pour the vegetable broth into a medium saucepan. Set over low heat to warm up.

2. Meanwhile, heat the olive oil in a large, high-sided skillet over medium heat. When the oil is shimmering, stir in the rice to coat completely in the oil, then smooth into an even layer. Cook, undisturbed, until slightly toasted, about 2 minutes.

3. Stir in the wine, chili paste, and oregano. Cook, stirring constantly, until the wine is dissolved, about 5 minutes. Start adding the warm broth, one ladleful at a time, and cook, stirring, until completely absorbed before adding the next, 20 to 25 minutes total. If your rice is too al dente for your taste and you've run out of broth, add hot water, ½ cup at a time, until it reaches your desired doneness.

4. Remove from the heat and stir in the butter and honey. Season with a big pinch of salt. Taste for seasoning, then pour the risotto onto a rimmed sheet pan and spread it into an even layer. Let cool completely, about 1 hour, then refrigerate for at least 2 hours to set.

5. **MAKE THE ARANCINI:** Line a rimmed sheet pan with parchment paper. Scoop 2 tablespoons of risotto and gently press into a ball. Set on the prepared sheet pan. Continue scooping and molding to make 12 balls, then refrigerate for 30 minutes.

6. In a shallow bowl, evenly spread out the flour. In a second shallow bowl, beat the eggs. In a third shallow bowl, evenly spread out the breadcrumbs. In a large Dutch oven fitted with a thermometer, heat the oil over medium heat to 375°F.

7. Meanwhile, working with one risotto ball at a time, roll it through the flour, then through the egg to coat, allowing any excess to drip off. Roll through the breadcrumbs, lightly pressing to adhere. Return to the parchment.

8. Working in batches, add a few balls to the oil and cook, turning occasionally, until golden brown, about 4 minutes, then transfer to paper towels to drain. Return the oil to 375°F between batches.

9. Arrange the hot arancini on a plate and dust with Parmesan and pepper flakes. Serve immediately.

Garlicky Broccoli Rabe

Serves 6 to 8

A steaming plate of garlicky broccoli rabe was a foundational part of Sunday dinner at Bimpy and Grandma Katherine's house. Broccoli rabe, the bitter cousin to broccolini (IDK what she's so mad about), offers a nice break to the otherwise decadent spread. This pile of greens, swimming in garlic and oil, is simple perfection. When I was a kid, you would find me piling my broccoli rabe onto a crusty piece of Italian bread and sprinkling lots of Parmesan on top. As an adult, you will still find me doing that, and I hope you will join me.

Kosher salt

2 bunches broccoli rabe

⅓ cup extra-virgin olive oil

8 garlic cloves, thinly sliced

Red pepper flakes

Block of Parmesan cheese, for serving

1. Bring a large pot of salted water to a boil over high heat. Add the broccoli rabe and cook, stirring occasionally, until vibrant green and almost tender, about 5 minutes. Drain in a colander and run under cold water to stop the cooking. Pat dry with paper towels.

2. In a large skillet, combine the olive oil and garlic. Set over medium-high heat, and cook, stirring occasionally, until the garlic just begins to brown, about 3 minutes.

3. Add the broccoli rabe and toss to coat. Smooth into an even layer and cook until the edges begin to crisp and the stems are cooked through, about 4 minutes. Remove from the heat and season with salt and pepper flakes before serving with Parmesan on the side for grating.

LASAGNETTA, PAGE 274

Lasagnetta

Serves 6 to 8

When I lived in San Francisco, my dear friend Julianne and I were regulars at an adorable Italian restaurant called Il Borgo. (It's still there; go visit!) The restaurant's cozy, homey décor, and friendly staff always made us feel like we were on a mini vacation to Italy. Our go-to order was the lasagnetta, a sort of conceptual lasagna roll-up. The good news is this stunning presentation doesn't require any more effort than building a regular lasagna, and I actually think it's more fun—like a craft project! You're still spreading a cheese mix over boiled noodles, but this time you're also layering on a slice of prosciutto and a fresh basil leaf and rolling the noodle up into a tight swirly spiral. A creamy tomato sauce awaits in the dish to simmer and seep in during the bake. Let's go, swirls!

Make Ahead The assembled lasagnetta can be covered with cling wrap and refrigerated up to 24 hours; bring to room temperature before baking.

Kosher salt

1 pound dried lasagna noodles

Extra-virgin olive oil

1 (28-ounce) can crushed tomatoes

½ cup heavy cream

4 garlic cloves

Freshly ground black pepper

8 ounces low-moisture mozzarella cheese, shredded

1½ cups whole-milk ricotta cheese

¾ cup freshly grated Parmesan cheese

8 ounces thinly sliced prosciutto, halved lengthwise

1 large bunch basil

---

1. Preheat the oven to 400°F.

2. Bring a large pot of salted water to a boil over high heat. Add the noodles and cook until al dente according to the package directions. Drain the noodles, then rinse under cold water to cool. Toss with olive oil to prevent sticking.

3. Meanwhile, in a blender, combine the tomatoes, ¼ cup of the heavy cream, and garlic, and season with salt and pepper. Blend on medium speed until smooth, about 1 minute. Taste for seasoning and add more salt and pepper as needed, then pour the sauce into a 9 × 13-inch baking dish.

4. In a large bowl, stir together the mozzarella, ricotta, Parmesan, and the remaining ¼ cup heavy cream. Season with salt and pepper.

5. Working with one at a time, lay down a lasagna noodle on a cutting board and cut it in half lengthwise. With the frilly edge facing away from you, spread 2 tablespoons of the cheese mixture onto each half. Lay a piece of prosciutto on the right side of each noodle, leaving some cheese exposed. Place a few basil leaves on top of the prosciutto. Roll up one of the noodles, working toward the exposed end; stop before it's fully rolled and slide the exposed end under the second noodle, lightly pressing to adhere. Continue rolling into one large spiral, then lightly press the other exposed end to seal. Place the spiral in the prepared baking dish with the frilly edge facing up. Continue slicing, filling, and rolling the noodles, using up the cheese, prosciutto, and basil, until 12 spirals are nestled in the sauce.

6. Bake the lasagnetta for about 30 minutes, until the sauce is bubbling and the top is beginning to brown in spots. Let cool for about 10 minutes to set before serving from the baking dish.

Pork Chops *with* Vinegar Peppers

Serves 6 to 8

This dish is made for the Carmela Soprano that lives in all of us. It's the type of cooking that makes you feel like a mob boss's wife—fabulous hair, perfect nails, and abundant food . . . maybe minus the crime. These pork chops are seared to golden perfection and smothered in a criminally flavorful sauce of onions, peppers, and a splash of vinegar, making every bite a savory masterpiece. It's the kind of flavor that even Carmela's mother-in-law would approve of.

Make Ahead *The seasoned pork can be refrigerated up to 48 hours (see Note).*

4 (1-inch-thick) bone-in pork chops

Kosher salt and freshly ground black pepper

2 tablespoons extra-virgin olive oil, plus more as needed

1 medium yellow onion, halved and sliced

1 (16-ounce) jar sweet or hot cherry peppers, drained

1 tablespoon all-purpose flour

½ cup dry white wine

½ cup low-sodium chicken broth

¼ cup white wine vinegar, plus more as needed

1. Pat the pork chops dry with paper towels. Season generously with salt and pepper.

2. Heat the olive oil in a large cast-iron or nonstick skillet over medium heat. When the oil is shimmering, add the pork chops. Cook until golden brown, about 4 minutes per side. Transfer to a plate and set aside to rest.

3. Add more olive oil to the skillet if it looks dry. Add the onion, peppers, and a pinch of salt. Cook, scraping up any browned bits from the bottom of the pan, until the onions begin to soften, about 4 minutes. Sprinkle with the flour and cook, stirring, until just toasted, about 1 minute. Stir in the wine, chicken broth, and vinegar. Nestle the pork chops back into the skillet and pour over any collected juices from the plate. Simmer until the sauce is thickened and the chops are cooked through, about 6 minutes, flipping the chops halfway. Transfer to a cutting board and let rest for 10 minutes.

4. Add ½ cup water to the skillet and cook over medium heat, whisking vigorously, until a glossy, rich sauce forms, 5 to 7 minutes. Remove from the heat. Taste for seasoning and add more salt, pepper, or vinegar as needed.

5. Arrange the pork chops on a serving platter, then spoon the sauce, onions, and peppers over the top. Serve immediately.

Note

You can cook the chops right away, but for extra-good flavor, set a wire rack over a rimmed sheet pan and place the seasoned chops on top. Refrigerate for at least 2 hours or up to 48 hours. Bring to room temperature before cooking.

PORK CHOPS WITH
VINEGAR PEPPERS,
PAGE 275

Struffoli

Serves 6 to 8

For most Italian American kids, making struffoli is a cherished memory. After mixing, rolling, cutting, and frying, you end up with a mound of little dough balls dripping in an orange honey syrup. But the best part is the rainbow sprinkles that add the perfect festive touch, making these sweet bites even sweeter. So gather up the fam and get ready to spill sprinkles all over your kitchen floor. Watching the struffoli fly off the platter like a proud nonna makes it all worth it, of course.

Make Ahead The dough can be tightly wrapped with cling wrap and refrigerated up to 48 hours.

1¼ cups sugar

3 large eggs

¼ cup extra-virgin olive oil

Zest of 1 orange

½ teaspoon baking powder

½ teaspoon kosher salt

3 cups all-purpose flour, plus more for rolling

2 quarts neutral oil

½ cup honey

Juice of 1 orange

Rainbow nonpareil sprinkles, for serving

1. In a large bowl, whisk the sugar and eggs. Whisk in the olive oil, orange zest, baking powder, and salt. Stir in the flour until a soft dough forms. Wrap the dough tightly with cling wrap and refrigerate for at least 30 minutes.

2. Lightly flour a work surface. Cut the dough into 8 equal pieces and keep covered. Working with one at a time, roll each piece into a 12-inch long rope. Cut the rope into 1-inch pieces and roll each piece into a ball. Set the balls on a floured surface while you roll the rest.

3. Fit a large Dutch oven with a thermometer, then add the oil. Heat over medium heat to 350°F. Working in batches, pile the struffoli into a spider strainer then gently lower into the hot oil. They'll sink at first, then pop to the surface. Cook, turning occasionally, until golden brown, about 3 minutes. Transfer to paper towels to drain. Return the oil to 350°F and repeat with the remaining struffoli.

4. In a small saucepan, combine the honey and orange juice. Warm over low heat until it's a runny liquid. Transfer the fried struffoli to a large bowl and pour over the honey mixture. Toss to coat well, then pile the struffoli onto a serving plate. Drizzle any extra honey mixture over the top, then shower with sprinkles. Serve immediately.

Nonna's Negroni

Serves 6 to 8

While I adore the flavor of a classic negroni, I don't drink much—so for years I've been searching for a nonalcoholic version that didn't just involve using nonalcoholic spirits. Enter my friend and cocktail master, John deBary, who brilliantly helped me crack the code with a common pantry ingredient: hibiscus tea! (Does it get more nonna than a tea bag?) This Nonna's Negroni features grapefruit juice for bitterness, Red Zinger tea bags for floral and tannic notes, a little sugar for sweetness, and black peppercorns for that subtle, satisfying burn.

Make Ahead The cooled, brewed tea can be refrigerated in an airtight container up to 2 weeks.

1 medium navel orange

1 tablespoon whole black peppercorns

1 tablespoon whole cloves

10 hibiscus tea bags, such as Red Zinger

½ cup sugar

2 (12-ounce) cans tonic water

1 cup unsweetened grapefruit juice

Ice, for serving

Orange wedges, for serving

1. Use a vegetable peeler to peel the orange, avoiding as much white pith as possible. In a small saucepan, combine the orange peel with the peppercorns, cloves, tea bags, and 2 cups cold water. Bring to a boil over high heat.

2. Add the sugar and cook, stirring, until dissolved, about 1 minute. Cover, remove from the heat, and let cool completely, about 2 hours. Strain the tea, discard the solids and tea bags.

3. To serve, in a large pitcher, stir together the tea, tonic water, grapefruit juice, and about 1 cup ice. Divide among rocks glasses filled with ice and garnish with orange wedges before serving.

Note

To make one serving, fill a rocks glass with ice. Pour 1 ounce of grapefruit juice, 2 ounces of the tea, and 3 ounces of tonic water and stir to mix. Garnish with an orange wedge.

Grossy's DAD'S Guide

ITALIAN AMERICAN *Slang*

If you're going to cook like a nonna, you better start talking like one, too. To help you out, I asked my dad, Tom, the quintessential old-school Italian American, to put together a list of all his favorite slang words. If you grew up with a nonna, a nonno (or a Bimpy), several aunts named Maria, Tonys of all ages, and more cousins than you can count, this will be a walk down memory lane. For everyone else, get ready to get educated.

MY DAD, TOM PELOSI

A fa napola
ah fah NAH-poh-lah
literally, go to Naples; figuratively, go to hell

Agita
AH-jee-tah
heartburn

Aspat
ah-SPAHT
wait

Bacouz
bah-KOOZ
bathroom

Cacuzz
kah-KOOTZ
pumpkin head, moron

Capisce
kah-PEESH
do you understand?

Centann
chen-TAHN
one hundred years, a wish for good health

Che peccad
keh peh-KAHD
what a sin, shame

Che putz
keh POOHTS
what a smell, stink

Chooch
chooch
jackass

Fac yee fata dui
fahch yee FAH-tah doo-ee
mind your business

Faccia brut
FAH-chah broot
ugly face

Fangul
fahng-GOOL
go f*ck yourself

••••••

Gabagool
gah-bah-GOOL
capicola, cured ham

••••••

Gavone
gah-VOH-neh
ignorant person

••••••

Gidrul
gee-DROOL
cucumber, stupid person

••••••

Ma che bella
mah keh BEH-lah
how beautiful

••••••

Ma che cozza fai
mah keh KOHT-sah fah-ee
what are you doing?

GRANDMA MILLIE

"BIG" GRANDMA PELOSI

Mopina
moh-PEE-nah
dish towel

••••••

Morta da fama
MOHR-tah dah FAH-mah
eating like you are about to die, a glutton

••••••

Paesan
pah-ee-ZAHN
fellow countryman

••••••

Prosciut
proh-SHOOT
prosciutto, cured ham

••••••

Rigott
ree-GOHT
ricotta, cheese

Scustamad
skoo-STAH-mahd
no manners

••••••

Stata zit
STAH-tah zeet
shut up

••••••

Stu gatz
stoo GAHTS
f*ck it

••••••

Stunad
stoo-NAHD
moron

••••••

Tusipatz
too-see-PAHTS
you're crazy

••••••

Venaca
veh-NAH-kah
come here

GRANDMA KATHERINE

Recipe Index

Recipes by Course

Recipes by Main Ingredient

More Parties

Another Birthday

Roasted Shrimp Cocktail 189

Roasted Asparagus with Parmesan Sauce 223

Charred Broccoli with Anchovy Vinaigrette 176

Kevin's Roast Chicken over Stuffing 137

Magic Seven-Layer Sundae Bar 242

Nonna's Negroni 280

· · · · · · · ·

Someone Said "Yes"

Grossy House Rolls with Chive Butter 128

A Very Large Caesar Salad 266

Roasted Squash with Crispy Chickpeas & Feta 114

Roast Salmon with Smashed Olives 169

Pignoli Cookies 150

Grapefruit Mule 241

Housewarming

Beany Bikini Dip 70

Sunshine Pasta 80

Two Kinds of Roasted Tomatoes with Burrata & Prosciutto 172

Melted Leek & Lemon Roast Chicken 34

Olive Oil & Pistachio Berry Crisp 233

Celery Mocktini 203

· · · · · · · ·

Brunch = Breakfast + Lunch

A Simple Green Salad with Shallot Dressing 220

Roasted Carrot & Sweet Onion Galette 132

Tomato Pie 79

Pineapple Fennel Pulled Pork Sliders 214

Blackberry Lemon Dutch Baby 104

My Best Friend Mary 87

· · · · · · · ·

Meet the Parents

A Very Green Minestrone 239

Garlicky Broccoli Rabe 270

Chicken Cordon Bimpy 180

Don't Tell Your Nonna About This Lasagna 136

Spice Cake with Brown Sugar Frosting 141

Book Club Meeting

Labneh Tzatziki 70

Autumnal Cheese Ball 110

Grilled Vegetable Sandwiches 259

Roasted Fig & Goat Cheese Parfaits 38

Grossy P's Arnie P 62

· · · · · · · ·

After the Kids' Sports Game

Mollie's Peanut Butter Dip 71

Coconut Shrimp with Spicy Peach Dip 206

Spinach & Artichoke Dip Pasta Bake 224

Marinated Steak Tips over Herby Rice 37

Chocolate Cream Pie for Bimpy 198

Watermelon Lime Slushie 72

· · · · · · · ·

Gender Reveal

Please stop!

Acknowledgments

One last tip: At the end of every party, it's important to thank everyone who attended, especially those who helped make it so fabulous in the first place!

To my Grossy Girls: Thank you for showing up to my party over and over again with endless enthusiasm, support, and understanding. I cannot wait to see all the parties that come from this book!

To Casey Elsass, for showing up first to the party, ready to do anything and everything to make sure it was a success. There is no one else I would rather bring a book into this world alongside.

To Gus Heagerty: Please refer to page 5.

To my family and friends, for showing me that every meal at the table can be made special simply because of who you are eating it with.

To my editor, Amanda Englander, for knowing exactly what *Let's Party* was (and what it was called) before I even told you I wanted to write it. And to the whole team at Union Square & Co. for your continued belief in me as one of your authors.

To my book agent, Eve Atterman, and my manager, Adam Krasner, for being the coolest chaperones at my party and making sure the vibes are always right. Big thanks to the teams at WME and Two West as well.

To my book designer, Laura Palese: Thank you for allowing me to crash your party of one and embarking on the most fun and fulfilling design journey together. GrossyPalese forever.

To my photographer, Johnny Miller: Thank you for your calm and confident presence on set. You made these parties come to life on the page in a way I could have only dreamed of.

To my food stylist, Jess Damuck: Thank you for the gorgeous art you made with my recipes and for the exceptional skill and integrity that you quietly weaved into our process. Thank you also to the rest of the food styling team, Dylan Going and Ben Weiner, for your dedication and meticulous work.

To my prop stylist, Randi Brookman Harris, for being a color and pattern celebrationist like me. Composing tablescapes with you was a singular experience that I enjoyed every second of. And to the rest of the props team, Elena and Joanna Sullivan, for all your tireless work.

To my wardrobe stylist, Eddie Oh, for using your brilliance to make everyone in this book look and feel exactly like themselves.

To my recipe testers, Sam Burros, Jacqui Tris, Ben Weiner (again), and John deBary, for taking these recipes into your care and making them better with your feedback and expertise.

To Eric King and Ben Weiner (once again!), for baking batches of classic Grossy holiday cookies in October without breaking a nail.

To Cath Heagerty, for your delicious pasta recipe and for once again letting me borrow your gorgeous table linens to include in this book.

To Kevin G. Bender, for always making the perfect roast chicken just when we all need it most.

To Ida Rose, my most trusted and honest recipe tester. If you didn't approve of a recipe, it didn't make it into this book!

To Jane McDonaugh, for letting me barge in at the drop of a hat to take over your kitchen when I didn't have one.

To Patrick and Steven, for allowing me to bask in your sunshine.

To the team at Random Harvest, for a summer of sandwiches and for your beautiful backyard.

A very big thank-you to every brand that generously donated their gorgeous products to this book. I am so lucky to have you all as part of my world:

ace&jig	Gap Inc.
Alex Mill	Geometry House
Atelier Saucier	Goldie Home
Block Shop Textiles	Great Jones
Caroline Z Hurley	Heath Ceramics
Crate & Barrel	Heather Taylor Home
Crow Canyon Home	Le Creuset
Dansk	MADRE Linen
Falcon Enamelware	Material Kitchen
Fireclay Tile	MoMA Design Store
Fishs Eddy	Schoolhouse x Claire V.
Food52	The Six Bells
Fredericks & Mae	Todd Snyder
Furbish Studio	YETI

Index

Note: Page references in *italics* indicate photographs.